"Pepper's direct yet compassionate guidance provides apt compensation for the short shrift our society often gives men in terms of self-awareness, empathy, and relationship communication. This book should be required reading for all straight or bi men seeking healthy relationships of any kind!"—Cunning Minx, creator of the *Polyamory Weekly* podcast

"Nonmonogamy has needed this book and didn't even know it. Pepper Mint offers gentle and frank advice for men who date women on how to ethically navigate nonmonogamy while being aware of power structures and gendered social norms. By addressing and guiding the reader through complex emotional labor, *Playing Fair* models how to be a supportive partner to women while being supportive to the reader."—Kitty Stryker, editor of *Ask: Building Consent Culture*

"A must-read book for the nonmonogamy community and those considering a foray into our world. As a woman who dates men, I may start requiring Pepper Mint's book of suggestions, detailed empathy-building opportunities, and tips for mutually satisfying sex to future partners!"—Katie Klabusich, writer, speaker, and radio host

"Everything you ever wanted to say to the single cis/het guy crashing the play party."—AV Flox, sex tech and science journalist for the *LA Times*, *Village Voice*, *LA Weekly*, *Vice*, and *Gizmodo*

"Pepper has, perhaps more than most, thought long and hard about how All This Stuff works. Here he addresses men looking to successfully do polyamory, and such people will find this book very rewarding. But so might anyone interested in excellent analysis of how any flavor of relationship works, because this book is not merely a set of rules ('do these steps and everything will work') but also goes deeply into the real-world contexts that generate the considerations offered here. It's not just the what, it's the why behind the what. Read this book to understand the why, and the 'what' steps follow naturally."—Barry Smiler, BmorePoly

"Whether you're new to nonmonogamy and trying to chart a course or an old hand trying to find a better route to your destination, *Playing Fair* is a brilliant road map for a more conscientious approach to ethical nonmonogamy."—from the foreword by Kevin Patterson, creator of *Poly Role Models* and author of *Love's Not Colorblind*

PLAYING FAIR

PLAYING FAIR

A GUIDE TO NONMONOGAMY FOR MEN INTO WOMEN

Pepper Mint

with a foreword by Kevin Patterson

 THORNAPPLE PRESS

Playing Fair
A Guide to Nonmonogamy for Men Into Women
Text copyright © 2017 by Pepper Mint
Foreword copyright © 2017 by Kevin Patterson

Thornapple Press
300 – 722 Cormorant Street
Victoria, BC V8W 1P8 Canada
press@thornapplepress.ca

Thornapple Press is a brand of Talk Science to Me Communications
Inc. and the successor to Thorntree Press. Our business
offices are located in the traditional, ancestral and unceded
territories of the ləkʷəŋən and W̱SÁNEĆ peoples.

Cover and interior design by Jeff Werner
Substantive editing by Alan MacRobert
Copy-editing by Hazel Boydell
Proofreading by Amy Haagsma

Library of Congress Cataloging-in-Publication Data
Names: Mint, Pepper, author.
Title: Playing fair : a guide to non-monogamy for men / Pepper Mint
Description: Portland, OR : Thorntree Press, 2017. |
    Series: Thorntree fundamentals
Identifiers: LCCN 2017016195 (print) | LCCN 2017034598 (ebook) |
    ISBN 9781944934392 (ePub) | ISBN 9781944934408 (Mobipocket) |
    ISBN 9781944934415 (Pdf) | ISBN 9781944934385 (paperback)
Subjects: LCSH: Non-monogamous relationships. | Families. | Interpersonal
    relations. | Love. | BISAC: FAMILY & RELATIONSHIPS / Love & Romance
Classification: LCC HQ980 (ebook) | LCC HQ980 .M56 2017 (print) |
    DDC 306.84/23--dc23
LC record available at https://lccn.loc.gov/2017016195

10   9   8   7   6   5   4   3   2

Printed in Canada.

CONTENTS

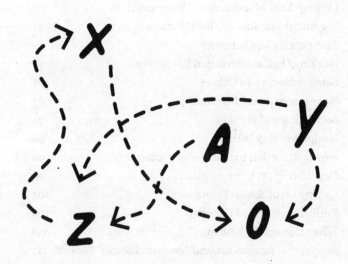

FOREWORD

At some point in my nonmonogamous journey, I discovered online dating. I stumbled out of the world of monogamy bass ackwards, pretty much by accident. So, I didn't have much of a path laid out in front of me. Away from the relationship that would eventually become my marriage, my dating pool was basically made up of my friend group. It was the only way I could be certain that all parties were aware that exclusivity wasn't an option. Of course, that severely limited my interactions to partners who were essentially killing time between monogamous relationships. I knew that I would have to branch out.

Through some combination of random occurrences, I came across OkCupid. Kasidie and AdultFriendFinder seemed centered on swinging. That's fine, but not what I was looking for. eHarmony and Plenty of Fish rejected me for being married, which was a condition I wasn't interested in changing. OkCupid was free, accepting of nonmonogamy, and full of people looking for relationships. I created a profile, answered a bunch of questions, and prepared to meet everybody. And then ... nothing.

What followed was several changes in approach, more profile rewrites than I can count, and at least one complete redo of the questions that determine the site's match percentage algorithm. I tried reading profiles thoroughly and sending thoughtful personally relevant messages.

I tried copying and pasting the same polite message to several prospects at once. In one shameful episode, I even attempted to neg someone. But no matter what adjustments I made, even at my most successful, I could never achieve more than minimal communication with the people I was attempting to woo.

When I got more involved in online polyamory communities, I was able to commiserate with tons of other men who had had similar experiences with online dating. Lots of attempts, very few responses. The highlight of that discovery was a guy looking for advice on Reddit. It was a fairly popular story at the time. An entitled young man used an ultimatum to pressure his girlfriend into a nonmonogamous relationship. He was then shocked to discover that, despite being mismatched by conventional beauty standards, her success in dating far outstripped his own. Like the guy on Reddit and many of the other men struggling with getting responses online, it was easy to place the burden of blame on the women we were dating and/or the women we were pursuing. Of course, it couldn't be our own ineptitude and women's tales of receiving never-ending streams of messages on online dating sites was just poking fun at our collective plight.

Margaret Atwood said, "Men are afraid that women will laugh at them. Women are afraid that men will kill them." I guess that's a concept that none of us stopped to consider. The idea that those we sought to engage with had a different but equally relevant set of experiences

just sort of escaped us. Oblivious, self-centered, male entitlement at its finest, right? Sometimes, that's what we're best at.

Had any of us bothered to lean out of our own myopic worldview, we'd have noticed blogs like *Nice Guys of OkCupid* on Tumblr or Instagram pages like Bye Felipe and Tinder Nightmares. We'd have listened to all of the stories about men who went from pleasant to creepy to violently dangerous as soon as things didn't go their way. We'd have believed those recounting and we'd have done something about it. Done something about our bros. Done something about ourselves.

In a monogamous society, it's easy to write off any responsibility for the way men treat dating prospects. It can literally be a wide world of every man for himself. But ethical nonmonogamy is smaller. Unlike with monogamy, we don't have lifetimes worth of parental examples and pop culture role models to serve as a template. Our tight-knit, often overlapping dating circles gather in discussion groups, online forums, and lifestyle conferences just to find others like ourselves. Just to prove to ourselves that we're not alone. We're forging new paths here, where every new step is someone's first step. We're bucking societal trends. So, if that's the case, let's buck this one as well. Let's get away from men being apathetic to the effect we have on the people we intend to date, love, or fuck. Let's stop pretending that we don't have a responsibility to those around us. We have to do better for ourselves, our partners, and our communities.

Playing Fair is exactly what is needed. My 15 years of trial and error would have contained significantly fewer missteps had I read this book. My next 15 will contain fewer still now that I've got it. Whether you're new to nonmonogamy and trying to chart a course or an old hand trying to find a better route to your destination, *Playing Fair* is a brilliant road map for a more conscientious approach to ethical nonmonogamy.

—Kevin Patterson, M.Ed., curator of *Poly Role Models*

INTRODUCTION

Hello! It is good to meet you, dear reader. Welcome to my book on nonmonogamy for men—specifically, men who are attracted to women.

Up to now, I have spent 14 years journeying in the world of nonmonogamy. Actually, that's how long I consider that I've been relatively successful at it. Before that were another 13 years of miserable failure. I have seen all kinds of good, bad, and ugly that alternatives to monogamy can bring.

In my own life, and in the sex-positive communities I belong to, I've seen a consistent theme: gender issues screw up nonmonogamy. By "gender issues" I mean conflicts created by our ideas of how women and men are supposed to be. As a man who mostly dates and sleeps with women, I have had to move past a number of ingrained attitudes about nonmonogamy, subtle entitlement issues, and bad gendered assumptions that the surrounding culture has handed us.

While such self-work is never done, making these changes has really worked out for me. For eight years now I have been getting everything I want from nonmonogamy. I have a number of partners, we are all happy with the relationships, and I stay connected with them while also raising a young child. I attend sex and play parties, and I play with women (and sometimes men and people of other genders) both in and out of these events. I can't imagine getting anything more out of my nonmonogamous romantic and dating life—I am happy and content. I am living the fantasy that a lot of straight guys wish for, but getting to this place was not easy. The problem with fantasies is that making them real often involves difficult change, hard work, and changing one's expectations.

I consistently see nonmonogamous men who are unhappy in their dating and sex lives. Some of this is just the difficulty of nonmonogamy itself in a monogamy-centric society: successful, ethical, happy nonmonogamy involves a lot of unlearning and relearning. But I also see gender issues: men fail to connect well with women, whether for hookups or deeper relationships. And it's often because of things these men bring to the table that they themselves don't understand.

Unexamined gender issues often lead to no dates. Or fewer dates. Or no second dates. Or potential dates who seem to fade into the woodwork after a promising start. All of these situations can happen without you knowing how you are sabotaging yourself and without knowing how you are making life harder for the women around you. A lot of men who want to be nonmonogamous mess it up because they cannot let go of gendered assumptions and habits—or even see them.

My goal is to empower you, dear reader, to make the changes in yourself and your practices that improve your nonmonogamous dating and relationship life. You already have the ability for great self-improvement. We all do.

This book will focus quite a bit on internal self-work, which I know is not a popular subject among men. Most guys would prefer a user's manual with the seven steps to assembling the dating-and-sex life of their dreams. But the steps that actually work are more subtle. They are straightforward enough once you grasp them, and while difficult at times, they are probably easier and more rewarding than you imagined.

Read on.

THEMES

Before we get started, let's lay out some concepts that will crop up repeatedly.

First: *Better people make better dates*. Better people make for better deep relationships and for better flings and better hookups. Better people are just more fun to be around. And, being better is actually the good and right thing to do. So how can we be better? This book will be a mix of practical nonmonogamy skills alongside the self-work of being a better person. The two go hand in hand: usually the best way to get the details right is to get the attitudes and assumptions right.

One aspect of being a better person is *being authentic*. Lots of guys speak and act in a straightforward manner, but often that straightforward manner serves to hide the deeper aspects of what is going on in our personalities. Our individualistic and macho cultures encourage men to suppress emotions, to take charge (sometimes through entitlement and coercion), and to bend the truth whenever it seems necessary to do so.

Being authentic means not just acting and expressing yourself directly, but also connecting with your own inner desires. This means knowing yourself in a way that many people do not. It means communicating effectively, caringly, and clearly. It means acting with integrity—no deceit or lies by omission—and being compassionate and generous.

Playing power games in relationships is the opposite of being authentic. Putting one's own needs ahead of others' or negotiating in bad faith are routes to relationship failure. Being authentic often means being vulnerable, both emotionally and also around personal power in relationships. Being vulnerable is new and difficult for many men. However, being authentic and vulnerable means that women can trust us and engage with us in cooperative problem-solving. This leads to much better relating, and more of it.

Another aspect of better people is that they *take responsibility*. Men are often encouraged to "take responsibility," but this gendered sense of responsibility is often oddly limited. Men are supposed to be responsible for laboring to earn money, but not for the labor found in successful personal connections—whether emotional labor, household labor, or even the labor of negotiating hookups or other sexual connections well. Our cultures often *encourage* men to be irresponsible when it comes to sex, relationships, and especially nonmonogamy.

Emotional labor is the work of caring for people, maintaining romance, helping others feel good, processing difficult emotions, talking through problems, helping people get along, keeping up friendly interpersonal connections, and so on. In dominant Western cultures men push women to perform most emotional labor. This is to our detriment, as this is the actual work of making relationships happen. A key piece of taking responsibility for our relationships is *taking on emotional labor*.

We have an association of nonmonogamy with freedom, and this leads guys to imagine that nonmonogamy means they can be less responsible. But that is exactly the wrong approach. Acting irresponsibly quickly leads to isolation. Responsibility and freedom go hand in hand in interpersonal connections, for the simple reason that connections involve other people. I am freer to engage with women in many ways (dating, sexually, in friendship, and so on), more than ever before in my life and this freedom *demands* responsibility and accountability.

One of the most important things to be responsible around is poisonous gender dynamics and unexamined entitlements. Bad gender expectations and power dynamics quickly sabotage nonmonogamous connections between men and women. Feeling entitled to unequal situations or power plays leads to disaster—and word gets around. I've seen the jealousy and emotional issues that arise from toxic masculinity make men undatable in nonmonogamous circles. *Letting go of sexism and entitlements* can be very hard, but the result is the reward of being a better person and, consequently, more and better connections.

The truth is, men have always had access to nonmonogamy in ways unavailable to women—that is, via mistresses, concubines, and sex workers. There is a theme to this: nonmonogamy for men has historically come from power over women. It has often been coercive and harmful, and has been particularly available to men with an excess of power and wealth.

Today we're seeing the birth of a new, egalitarian nonmonogamy: where women are full and valued participants with the personal agency to choose nonmonogamy for themselves. Its forms include polyamory, swinging, open relationships, and relationship anarchy. This is great for women, and can be great for men. Modern nonmonogamy is a party everyone is invited to. But for men in particular, the price of entry is shedding double standards, entitled attitudes, and other bad habits of masculinity.

And that leads to our final theme: it is important to *treat women well*. This does not mean well as in "put her on a pedestal and worship her," but well as in "treat her with the humanity and respect that every person has by right."

In our sexist culture, and in nonmonogamous communities that are saddled with a sexist background, treating women well turns out to take much more attention, effort, and self-work than one might expect.

Part of treating women well is getting away from objectification: the various ways we treat women as not-fully-human *objects* rather than as *people*. For both moral and practical reasons, we must treat women as people first, and as potential sex and relationship targets later, if at all. Making sure that the women in our lives have agency and respect is crucial to good living and being a better person.

Beyond that, it is important to find ways to *support the women in our lives in their struggles*. This includes those struggles that result from sexism, sexist men, and a sexist culture. There are various words for this: feminism, anti-sexism, or just being a decent person. They all boil down to recognizing that women face problems in our culture that men don't. It is important to correct that imbalance and support women.

Treating women with respect requires that we *learn to listen to women*. We come from an unfortunate cultural background that encourages men to ignore or even try to silence women's concerns. What a woman wants is often particular to the person or the situation, and the only way to find out is to ask. We must listen to our women partners and women in our communities to create the nonmonogamous world we desire.

There is also the question of your motivation. I'm aware of talking about all these ways we can be better people in a book on nonmonogamous dating. To truly be a better person, one must commit to that for its own sake, not to reap the (very real) rewards these changes bring in a nonmonogamous environment. Otherwise your changes will be shallow and meaningless. Let me tell you, women can smell that shit a mile away. If you cannot make the commitment to self-improvement for its own sake, put this book down now—I cannot help you.

But if you *can* make that commitment, I have all sorts of ideas and directions that will be useful.

To recap, here are our themes. Watch for them as we move forward:

→ Being a better person
→ Being authentic
→ Taking responsibility
→ Taking on emotional labor
→ Letting go of entitlements
→ Working on sexist conditioning
→ Treating women as people rather than things
→ Supporting women against sexism
→ Listening to women

SCOPE AND DISCLAIMERS

This book is addressed to men who are attracted to women—typically men who identify as straight or bisexual. I use language specifically for them. I do this both because I am speaking from my own experience and because I see that the issues men bring to nonmonogamy are the source of most problems in mixed-gender nonmonogamous communities. It is not my intent to erase the experiences of trans, nonbinary, or gender-nonconforming people—I am personally in the latter group.

As you have probably noticed, this book has a lot of gender generalizations in it. Generalizations are often wrong for specific people. If a statement does not fit with your life or experience, please ignore it and move on.

These gender generalizations should not be read as claiming that women or men are naturally a certain way. I do not believe there is any more real or more natural way to be a man or woman or innately masculine or feminine behavior. The actual experiences of being a woman or a man (or a girl or boy) end up being different due to the cultural norms around us, and those differences lead to different attitudes and behaviors on average. Indeed, generalizing is often necessary to address or improve gendered patterns of behavior in the culture, and that is what I am trying to do here.

I refer to romantic and/or sexual connections by varying terms: partner, connection, relationship, hookup, and so on. I use these terms pretty much interchangeably. While there are definitely differences between how one approaches a long-term relationship and how one approaches a hookup, the advice in this book is designed to be applicable across the spectrum of connections. Also, many nonmonogamous people are asexual, not interested in romance, or seeking nonstandard connections such as platonic co-parenting. As you read, please consider my advice in light of all different sorts of connections.

The lessons and directives in this book are based on my own experience, which is by no means universal. I am trying to point out common patterns I see and relevant solutions. Your experience and predilections may make a particular piece of advice irrelevant to you, and that is okay.

The experience I speak from is grounded in my own cultural location: United States, white, male, hetero-sexual-ish, middle to upper class, liberal, urban, mostly able-bodied, mostly cisgender, and so on. The advice may become less relevant the farther you are from these cultural locations—whether you are in a subculture or minority culture, or come to this advice from a totally different cultural background.

This book looks at how gender dynamics mess up relationships, but gender is only one piece of the puzzle. Someone more qualified than me could (and should!) write an entire book on how racial power dynamics screw up non-monogamous relationships. Same for classism, ableism, and so on.

I'm certainly not claiming to be perfect, or to be an authority on nonmonogamous perfection. I have had numerous problems in my nonmonogamous journey, and some of them are ongoing. I speak from a position of learning from my mistakes and failures.

The primary term I use for the subject of this book is "nonmonogamy." I consider this an umbrella term for polyamory, swinging, open relationships, relationship anarchy, and so on. My own experience is in polyamorous communities and pansexual sex parties (and not really in swinger parties). Still, I feel that the principles I lay out here will apply to most nonmonogamous experiences most of the time. Because monogamy is highly consistent across our culture, forms of resistance to monogamy will also be fairly consistent, even when they come in different communities with different languages and norms.

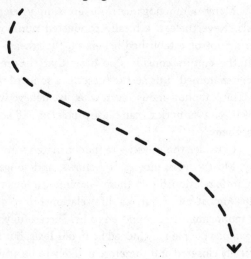

LETTING GO OF MONOGAMOUS MISCONCEPTIONS

As it turns out, the biggest obstacle to being nonmonogamous is ... monogamy. Or rather, the monogamous baggage we all carry.

Many nonmonogamy skills are simply relationship skills. Nevertheless, ethically conducted nonmonogamy turns a lot of established beliefs on their head—things that the culture considers so basic that they're mostly never examined. This section describes some of the ways we "think monogamous" even when we believe we don't, how these assumptions can cause problems, and how to get past them.

Consider the ways we're indoctrinated into monogamy. Most novels, movies, TV shows, and songs have a romantic relationship in them—a monogamous relationship. Almost all of our real-life relationship role models are monogamous or supposed to be. Successfully nonmonogamous people may indeed be in our lives, but they are typically closeted and therefore unlikely to be available as role models.

Everyone assumes that people pair off in couples. Invites to gatherings are usually "plus one"—that is, your one "significant other" and no one else. Socializing is built around couples, singles, or a mix of the two. Consider insurance plans and immigration law. All business and government models assume at most one other partner.

Monogamous assumptions are woven into our thinking about love and romance, long-term commitment, successful partnerships, handling of household finances, sexual fulfillment, and so on. Sexual monogamy became a formal marriage requirement centuries before most of our other relationship concepts came into existence. So we come to nonmonogamy loaded with hidden monogamous assumptions. Let's unearth some of those assumptions.

COLLABORATION INSTEAD OF COMPETITION

In the monogamous world, love and sex are assumed to be scarce commodities. Many difficulties arise from this imposed economics of scarcity.

It starts with the fact that most people are already in relationships and therefore unavailable. Even in a relationship, love and sex are only available from that one other person. This is fine for people who actually want to be monogamous, but limiting and potentially traumatizing for others. Among single people even the *possibility* of a relationship with a new person is fraught with high-stakes peril due to fear of isolation or missed opportunities.

This scarcity mentality sets up a highly competitive situation for sex and romance. People sometimes find themselves shut out of dating almost entirely. This is particularly true if they are in a nonnormative or oppressed group—someone whose potential partners may balk at the stigma they face, whether transphobia, racism, fatphobia, ableism, or other. Even for those who are successful in the dating market, the competitive aspect of monogamy leads people to take actions of questionable morality, such as cheating or "trading up" to a more desirable partner.

Most people bring this competitive attitude when they start exploring nonmonogamy. This is particularly relevant to men competing with other men, though women are competitive as well. There's an attitude that other men should be distrusted and undermined at every opportunity, especially men who are relationship rivals. Of course this leads to drama and discord. We see a lot of bad practices sprout from this competitiveness, such as "one penis policy" relationships, where a man is allowed to see multiple women but those women are discouraged from seeing other men.

Unlike monogamy, successful nonmonogamy consistently tends to be collaborative, not competitive. Certainly the nonmonogamous dating scene can sometimes feel competitive. However, because most people in it are open to new connections and everyone knows it, dating opportunities are available to most.

Cooperation is how people get along and build connections. In nonmonogamy, *supporting your partners' connections with other people is fundamentally a good idea* that strengthens your own relationships. The happier your partners are in their other connections, the more fulfilled they are in general, and the happier they are with you.

So it is important to let go of competitiveness and think of yourself as on the same team as the rest of your relationship network.

This means not setting up rules that are harmful to other relationships or connections. And it definitely means not putting effort into competing with or trying to scuttle your partners' other connections. You should try to meet your partners' other lovers, and find ways to be generous to those connections. Maybe that means giving up the house for an evening so others can play. Maybe it means letting someone know that you consider their relationship with your partner to be valuable. Maybe it means inviting your partner's partner into your life in some meaningful way.

For most of us, this requires retraining. It is a skill to develop. You should consider the health of your nonmonogamous network to be important and worthy of your time, support, and encouragement. If there is drama in your network, it will probably negatively affect you. If things go well in your network, things will get better for you. Act to support the relationships and people in your network and you will find yourself with much more stability and abundance in your nonmonogamous life.

RESPONSIBILITY WITH FREEDOM

Another piece of monogamous ideology is the false dichotomy between freedom and responsibility. They are not opposites; they are tightly interdependent. Behave irresponsibly, and your freedom will evaporate. Behave well to others, and your freedom will expand and flourish.

We're raised to think of monogamous marriage as the epitome of responsibility via tropes like "for better or for worse" and "the old ball and chain." This does us a number of disservices.

First, it positions nonmonogamy as both freeing *and* irresponsible. See the problem? If people assume that going nonmonogamous means a no-holds-barred free-for-all, they will usually fail.

Second, relationship responsibility gets associated with resentments, as in phrases like "ball and chain." This hides the fact that responsibility is a good thing that gets you places.

Men in particular seem to be very susceptible to this way of thinking. I have met many nonmonogamous men who were resistant to anything resembling expectations or responsibility, even in little ways. I constantly see men who fail to show up, to make even small promises, or to return phone calls. Men often carry the false dichotomy between having fun and building connection, between getting what you want and doing the work to get it.

Some men see avoiding responsibility as a way of taking power for themselves—that is, as an aggressive way of signaling that they can do whatever they want. Such men end up doing whatever they want...alone.

I think that pornography tends to make this attitude worse. In mainstream porn, sex with no strings is the norm—women just walk into a situation and bang the pizza delivery guy. This is not the fault of porn—the genre just reflects the entitled male fantasy of unfettered sexual access to women. But that fantasy is rarely realized. Chances are it will never happen to you. Nevertheless, I have met many men who were on some kind of quest to find the magical land of easy women, where you just walk in the door and hot women throw themselves on you. These men jump from scene to scene looking for their fantasy and never find it. This is because in reality, women are *people* rather than sexual objects. People have their own desires and are picky in their own way, so connecting with them requires mutual attraction, negotiation, and consideration—not a self-centered fantasy.

Responsibility enables what I call "effective freedom," that is, the freedom to do what you want in the context of working with other people. It is important to learn how to welcome other people's desires and expectations, and to work with them cooperatively to build connection. This is true even for relatively lightweight connections. This was a very hard step for me to take, but once I did I found that my nonmonogamous sexual and relationship life blossomed.

As I started doing this work, women started being much more interested in being with me and staying with me. Try to start associating personal responsibility with positive freedom—the freedom to date women in a way that works.

WOMEN AS NONMONOGAMOUS

Another cultural myth is that women are inherently monogamous. Cultures created this myth to control women's sexuality—to keep women from sleeping around or otherwise owning their own sexual freedom. It also enables the wider control of women. That said, there is a more complex secondary layer to this myth as well.

The Western myth of women as monogamous started in the Victorian era, when sex work (the non-pejorative term for prostitution) was common and, dependent on place and time, legal. The women considered to be monogamous were only a *certain kind* of women—that is, "respectable" women in the gentry and newly established middle class. In short, the ones you were supposed to marry or at least aim to marry. The other type of women were sex workers and "loose women," often conflated with working class women, those in the "underclass," and women of color. This developed into what is known as the Madonna/whore complex: the idea that women are either sexually pure and uninterested in sex, or out-of-control immoral sluts. Dominant Western culture still tends to stereotype women as one or the other: highly sexual or nonsexually romantic. In reality, most women are some-where in the middle—they are people who, like most men, look to connect (sexually, romantically, both, or otherwise) only in particular situations.

From the Madonna stereotype, many of us get the idea that the nonmonogamy we want is impossible with the women we want to build a life with, or that we have to trick or force them into it. On the whore side of the dichot-omy, we tend to imagine that nonmonogamous women are hypersexual, out of control, and easily available. Both myths harm women because they lead us to not respect women's sexual agency. When moving into nonmonogamy, it is crucial to see these myths and shed them.

A lot more women are interested in nonmonog-amy than mainstream culture would have you believe. The number of women is similar to the number of men. Nonmonogamous women are in it for their own reasons: freedom to connect, multiple relationships, and so on. Their complex desires lead to complex negotiations, which then lead to situations where hopefully everyone is getting what they are looking for.

Never assume that a woman is available to you because she is nonmonogamous with others. Do not assume that she is sexually free or sexual at all—just as with men, some nonmonogamous women are asexual. Likewise, do not assume that she was somehow tricked into nonmonogamy or does not actually want it. Further, do not assume that she will oppose *your* nonmonogamous desires or, conversely, that she will want commitment and a deep emotional connection from you. You get the idea. Cultural ideas and assumptions around women and nonmonogamy are poison and will lead you astray. Let go of this cultural noise.

THE EMOTIONAL JOURNEY INTO NONMONOGAMY

The journey out of the monogamous world is not easy or quick for most people. It is not just a matter of letting go of old ideas. Intellectual adaptation as described above is the easy part of the work. The harder part is figuring out how to manage a lifetime of monogamous emotional conditioning—your emotional triggers and gut assumptions that still lie in wait. This cultural indoctrination can show up as jealousy, shame, guilt, anxiety, anger, withdrawal, or fear.

There are various approaches to handling these emotions and attempting to move past them. Sometimes this means doing the work to figure out what incorrect ideas or assumptions underlie your emotions and triggers, and addressing those. Other times it means finding past traumas or childhood issues that are being triggered and dealing with those directly. It may require that you or others learn to manage difficult feelings and avoid particular triggering situations. Sometimes it just takes time and learning to trust in other people. This section is devoted to describing some of this emotional work.

LEARNING FROM OTHERS

My first piece of advice: really do the research. The skill set you need is likely deeper and harder to learn than you think. Doing as much up-front learning as you can will smooth the process.

The polyamory community seems to specialize in creating resources for learning. Some books to take a look at are *The Ethical Slut, More Than Two, Opening Up,* and *The Jealousy Workbook.* There are many others. If you live in or near a city in a Western country, chances are there are nonmonogamy workshops and discussion/support groups happening near you. Bigger conferences are less common but still pretty easy to find—look for conferences labeled polyamory, open relationships, and swinging. There are numerous online resources including podcasts, discussion forums, blogs, and other free sources of support and education. You are very lucky to be entering nonmonogamy in a time with an incredibly large resource base. Use it.

This brings up an important point. Men are indoctrinated into a harmful myth of individualism when it comes to self-work, especially emotional self-work in relationships. Western culture leads us to believe that we already know this stuff, that we should just wing it, that it is more women's responsibility than ours, and that relationships will magically go well if people are truly meant to be together. These ideas are false, especially when learning an entire new relationship format. Yet men entering nonmonogamy are often unwilling to learn from others (say, by attending workshops), to work on their own emotional journey, or to generally do emotional labor. *Men tend to push emotional labor onto the women in their lives.* This attitude makes your journey longer and harder and more likely to fail.

So do the reading. Attend the workshops, discussions, and conferences if you have the financial means. Use the free resources if you don't. Talk to people who are doing it well and see what they tell you. Make plans and timelines to do self-work and have hard conversations with your partner(s). Follow the boundaries and expectations established in these conversations. Drop the conceited assumption that you already know everything—I can assure you that you do not.

Instead, approach these resources and this new knowledge with humility and curiosity. Really listen to what experienced people are telling you, even if (especially if) it conflicts with what you expect.

THE NONMONOGAMY TIMELINE

The journey into nonmonogamy usually takes longer than you expect. Expect the actual process to take six months to two years before you develop a base level of comfortable practice. Even people who are naturally low in jealousy or otherwise naturally nonmonogamous tend to get blind-sided as they learn new ideas and skills.

So plan to take it slowly. Beware the beginner's kid-in-a-candy-shop pattern: it can mess up your life. When people are too eager, disaster usually strikes quickly. Only then do they retrace their steps and think about getting help and working through things.

Keep in mind that six-month to two-year timeline. If you are opening a previously monogamous relationship, both of you should plan out a gradual approach where first you flirt with and kiss others, discuss how this goes, and then steadily but slowly move further to other activities. During this time, be sure to be honest and up front with new people about any limits and where you are at in your journey.

If you are starting from singlehood, begin any new connections with a discussion that you are nonmonogamous and will not be changing this. Be aware that you will likely run into some rocky periods at the three- to six-month mark in each relationship, as your connections deepen and you grapple with your new reality.

However, do not take things too slowly! And do not entirely compromise away your nonmonogamy, even for a while. It is easy to end up effectively monogamous even if that is not your intention. I have known people who were (and are) stuck in the "Let's try to open our relationship" phase for decades. You are looking for steady progress. Make a timeline and put it on a calendar, while understanding that it is common to halt or backtrack a bit.

If you do not seem to be moving forward within six months, it is time to look at the situation and possibly shake things up. If you're in a couple, you may face a choice between committing back to monogamy or breaking up. Be ready to face that possibility.

I encourage newly nonmonogamous people to connect with folks with more experience—those who are past the difficult first two years. This is true whether you are looking for relationships, hooking up at sex parties, or just talking to people. Having experienced people around to show you the ropes makes the transition much easier.

If you are lucky enough to date more experienced nonmonogamous women, you should *listen to them* and take their advice. I have seen numerous men think they knew better than their experienced partners, but they did not, and disaster followed. Be wise and take advantage of the wisdom of women in your life.

At the same time, not every experienced person has good skills or habits, so their advice may be bad. Worse, some longtimers use their experience as leverage to trap newbies into abusive or controlling situations. Do not depend on a single person for guidance—you're looking for a community, not just one mentor.

HANDLING HARD EMOTIONS

Jealousy.

The most common hard emotions on this journey are *jealousy* and *fear* centered on lovers seeing other people. Jealousy usually springs from fear—people are afraid of losing their partners to other people. It can arise regardless of whether you believe there's an actual threat. Jealousy often crops up in weird and surprising ways—people often expect it in certain circumstances but instead, it hits them unexpectedly in others.

The first step to handling jealousy is to be honest about what you are feeling. This is not a time to bottle up your feelings and try to tough it out. Suppressed emotions usually come out in ways that will be worse for you and everyone around you. It's best to open up and be emotionally vulnerable. Say things like "I am feeling jealous" or "I am feeling afraid." Or maybe you are less precise in your self-understanding and can only say "I seem to get upset when this happens." In any case, try to say as much as you can about what you are feeling, at whatever level of self-knowledge you may have around it.

Once you are openly talking about your emotional state, use that as a starting point for figuring out what's going on behind those emotions. Jealousy is famous for masking other emotions. *Why* are you feeling jealous? If you are afraid, what real-world scenarios are you afraid of? Unpacking your emotional responses will often reveal easy solutions. Maybe your fears just need some reassurance from your partner. Maybe any insecurities you have about the connection can be addressed directly, making you more confident about it. Or maybe you have a genuine external problem and your fears are justified.

Emotions can be stubborn, especially when they're based in your personal history. Try to talk through these emotions in various contexts, such as in sharing groups, with trusted nonmonogamous friends, or with a sympathetic therapist. If the source of an emotion is unclear, note *when* it tends to come up; this will often give you clues. Compare your emotional reaction to your history—is there some trauma or childhood pattern that established certain reactions or triggers? Understanding the emotion gives you the tools to handle it, divert it, avoid it, or manage it. Learn emotional management tools from therapy, from self-help books, or from other resources.

Learning to avoid secondary fear *of* the emotion can be a useful tool. That's when you become afraid of your own reactions. After a hard jealous fit or two, someone might become scared of their own jealousy and set up a lot of rules or other avoidance techniques to try to keep it from happening again. This sort of trigger avoidance is often not sustainable longterm. Instead, try to take ownership of the emotional reaction and purposefully put yourself in situations where it will come up. Do so in small steps, with the support of people around you, and in ways where you are still taking care of yourself. But do it. *Deprogramming uncomfortable emotions requires purposefully engaging with the discomfort.* If you find that you can go through an emotionally triggering situation and come out mostly fine on the other side, a lot of the secondary fear of the emotion will dissipate. Often, engagement leads to the emotion disappearing entirely.

Other tough feelings that crop up in nonmonogamy are tied to cultural myths or history. Deprogramming them requires getting away from monogamist and sexist cultural roots.

Possessiveness.

For a lot of known human history men basically owned women. Women went directly from being the property of their father to being the property of their husband. It was rare for women to be successfully independent. In particular, women's sexuality and ability to procreate was thought to belong to their husband—rape in marriage was legal, birth control was restricted, and so on.

Thankfully, we no longer live in that world. Now women and men meet as relative equals, and the resulting relationships have the potential to be much more fulfilling. Still, we carry echoes of that past. One is the continuing belief that we somehow own the sexuality of our partners. Modern monogamy is in many ways an echo of earlier outright possession.

If you want your nonmonogamy to succeed, *let go of any sense of ownership* over your partners—over their sexuality, attention, time, and choices. You will still have expectations and make agreements. But modern non-monogamy is composed of people who make their own decisions and who typically make their own connections.

You cannot honor this while still believing that you some-how own a woman, in whole or in part. Do the emotional work to let go of any sense of ownership.

Shame and guilt.

Another common feeling that nonmonogamy provokes is *shame*. This is no surprise—the stigma is huge. Dominant culture generally assumes that a nonmonogamous person is automatically immoral, dirty, selfish, carnal, diseased, unreliable, mentally unstable, and unfit for marriage or child-rearing. These associations are illogical but still per-sist. Once again, history is to blame; the stigmatization of nonmonogamy has historically been used to keep women's sexuality under control.

When we internalize such messages, one result is shame. This shame comes in two flavors: shame about ourselves, and shame about our partners.

Shame about ourselves tends to show up as *guilt*. People who get into nonmonogamy often start feeling guilty even if they are intellectually fine with it. Even suc-cessfully nonmonogamous people will often feel like they do not deserve to have what they have.

You can defuse this guilt. First and foremost, you should get the explicit approval of your partners to do the things you want to do with other people. This is true even if you have an agreement that you don't *need* this permission. If your partners are enthusiastically positive about your other connections, it will help free you from the idea that you are hurting or betraying them. It's even better if your partners or lovers meet and get along. Having everyone interact in a friendly and positive way really defuses anxieties or guilt we may feel about nonmonogamy. If a partner consistently says, "Yes, please go see her! That would be great!" then it's hard to feel you are doing them a disservice.

If your partners are *not* enthusiastic, positive, or willing to meet your other lovers, you need to re-evaluate. You cannot require them to be. Slow down and give them time as you work on this together. You want your nonmonogamous practice to be enthusiastic, positive, and socially integrated—doing anything else will, at the very minimum, wear you down. Getting there may take much time and emotional work. Accept this.

You may have a partner who wants to be nonmonogamous but is having hard emotions around it. In this situation, it is important to just try to let any guilt go and respect the agency of your partners. If they say they want this hard situation, then that is their decision, and not on you. This does not mean you should be crass or purposefully hard on them, or say they are doing it wrong and need to shape up. You should be supportive, but if someone has freely made a choice to be nonmonogamous with you, respect that choice by not taking that guilt onto yourself, even if nonmonogamy is currently difficult for them.

The other-person version of shame shows up in subtly shaming our partners or people we know, especially *slut-shaming* women. Women have been subject to millennia of slut-shaming, so it unfortunately comes easily and sometimes unconsciously. I see this all the time. Men find it easy to play on the residual guilt women may feel. Or to drop into the double standard, where it is okay for men to have other sexual partners but not for women. But shaming the women in your life, even subtly and unconsciously, will quickly sink your nonmonogamous practice and cause women to avoid you. Instead, do the opposite. Be clearly supportive of nonmonogamous women in your life and support their nonmonogamous practice.

If you have difficult emotions around this, one technique is to preface discussions with "I really want non-monogamy and I want to support your nonmonogamy" or similar statements. Similarly, be as positive, enthusiastic, and engaged as you can around their other connections, just like you would like them to be for yours.

Do the emotional work so you can easily meet and be comfortable around your partners' partners. Find ways to be generous and support those connections; remember that *the health of the relationship network affects the health of your own connections*. Being generous might mean giving up the occasional date night or making it into a group outing with your partner's partners. It may mean loaning them your car or guest bedroom, or even finding ways to share finances. You can also put in emotional labor to support these connections, maybe by giving advice or providing a shoulder to cry on, or perhaps by having your own friendly connection to your partners' partners, and providing support to them just like you would any other friend.

Emotions in low-involvement connections.
In these discussions of emotional issues, people tend to assume that they only arise in highly involved relationships, what many people call "primary" relationships. But difficult emotions can show up in any sort of connection.

Sometimes people are fine with their live-in partner's nonmonogamy but then find themselves jealous about a more casual lover's. It might not make sense to spend hours processing difficult emotions with someone you only see for a couple hours once in a while. But a kind of emotional shorthand develops. In lightweight connections, *it is important to state directly what is happening.* If you are feeling uncomfortable or having other hard issues, quickly and directly say so. If something goes wrong for you, or goes well, say that too. People engaged in lightweight connections tend to appreciate direct communication and clarity. Apologize in a straightforward way if you do something harmful, and so on. Learning to step away from silence and into courage and directness is sometimes easier with people you don't see very much or have a strong connection with. Bring effort to all your relating, including less-involved connections.

NONMONOGAMOUS TRAUMA AND DISTRUST

Beyond what we've discussed, there's often a background issue that I think of as "nonmonogamous trauma."

People who come to nonmonogamy have often wanted to live this way for a long time, but their culture keeps forcing them back into monogamy. The fact is, most uninformed forays into nonmonogamy go horribly wrong. So people often experience a long period of being "lost in the wilderness," stigmatized and blocked. This trauma shows up later in subtle and not-so-subtle ways.

Most obviously, we often have trouble trusting that our partners are actually, really interested in nonmonogamy and are enthusiastically willing to support us. Monogamous people are often willing to be nonexclusive at the beginning of a relationship but later demand exclusivity, regardless of what you told them and what they agreed to at the outset. A couple of bad experiences like this can make a person really distrust others' supposed interest in nonmonogamy. In addition, we are conditioned to believe that women are *never* interested in nonmonogamy. Many once- or twice-burned nonmonogamous men get that idea solidly stuck in their heads.

This *basic lack of trust* leads to other problematic behaviors. I see this so much. Men will refuse to negotiate around their nonmonogamy at all. They will disappear or stay out of contact in order to exert a kind of control over the situation. Or they will try to keep everything highly compartmentalized and make sure lovers are not aware of each other, possibly lying to do so. People may turn to manipulation and control—also known as abuse. All of this leads to problems in connection, because basic distrust will scuttle any connection. This lack of trust can become a self-fulfilling prophecy, causing people to trust even less.

A successful nonmonogamous journey requires digging oneself out of this. We need to learn to trust the women in our lives who actually want nonmonogamy for us and for themselves. It took me years to trust that the women I was dating were actually okay with my nonmonogamy, and more years to trust that some of them matched me in their particular nonmonogamous desires and styles. Do better than I did, and open your heart to the reality that there are nonmonogamous women who are absolutely on the same page as you. It is just a matter of finding them and learning to engage with them. Journeying to a place of trust will open up all sorts of possibilities for you: collaboration rather than deceit, successful negotiation to fulfill your desires, and an abundance of dating opportunities.

ATTEMPTING TO CONTROL NONMONOGAMY

When people feel these difficult emotions, they commonly respond by trying to control the situation. If someone is feeling jealous, insecure, or distrustful, they may try to stop their partners' activities with others. If someone is feeling unsafe, they may try to structure their nonmonogamy in a way that feels safer to them, though often such structures do not create actual safety. Men in particular try to exert control when stressed, or perhaps men are simply more likely to feel they have a right to control their partners.

However, *attempts at control cannot create healthy relationships*, and in the worst case lead to abusive relationships. Many first attempts at nonmonogamy fall apart due to unworkable rules or restrictions that seemed like a good idea at the time.

There are healthier ways to change a situation to help you feel safe. You can negotiate together in good faith to get your needs met and find ways to address any problems. This section is devoted to common mistakes that arise from the urge to control. I see them again and again.

Double standards.

The most obvious mistake is trying to institute a double standard: "I can do x but you can't." This is often "I can see other women, but you can't see other men." This is clearly unfair, but men often feel entitled to unfairness. However, double standards are a recipe for failure. Modern women have been promised egalitarian relationships and fair treatment, and that's what they expect. If your nonmonogamy is unfair, it will probably collapse.

And yet almost half the men I speak to who are new to nonmonogamy have some kind of double standard as part of their fantasy. Such ideas swiftly collide with reality.

These guys either manage to grow into a more egalitarian plan, or they fail at nonmonogamy. Some jump from relationship to relationship, seeking to impose control and failing each time.

One common example is a rule that the man can date other women but the woman or women involved can *also* only date women in addition to this man. In polyamory circles this is ridiculed as a "one penis policy." Eventually the unfairness wears on the women, especially if they have no interest in bisexuality, and they demand change or the relationship goes sour. If a one penis policy is your fantasy, let it go now. These arrangements have a deservedly terrible reputation in nonmonogamous communities, and most women will refuse to engage with such men.

A similar structure that men sometimes desire is dating several monogamous women, all of whom will be monogamous to him alone. But guess what? Monogamous people are interested in ... monogamy. And they are rarely flexible about it. You are not what they want.

Similarly, in kink circles I have often seen men try to set up dominance/submission (D/S) relationships where they, as the dominant partner, get to see multiple people, but the submissives they are dating cannot. The excuse is that a submissive's nonmonogamy would somehow break the D/S dynamic. A lot of kink fantasies (say chastity play) do include control over a partner's sexuality, so people can use it to excuse the old double standard. But monogamy versus nonmonogamy is one of those base relationship elements that needs to be determined outside of the D/S dynamic. Or to put it differently, one cannot submit one's way out of jealousy or into a desire to be nonmonogamous.

One way people can craft a double standard is to set up nonmonogamy rules that are equal only on the surface. One penis policies are an example: *everyone* gets to date women but not men—regardless of what the women want. But unequal rules can come in subtler forms. Whenever a supposedly equal rule actually allows one person to get what they want while restricting another, it is not really equal.

For example, suppose a couple has a rule that their only outside connections are no-strings hookups at sex parties. That would hardly be fair if one member of the couple wants no-strings hookups and the other wants more emotional or connected relationships. Be careful that your "equal" rules enable everyone to get what *they* want in equal measure.

Often people use manipulative tactics to enforce a double standard. Examples include changing rules every week (open! closed! open!) depending on who's managing to get a date, or using a veto rule selectively against the relationships that one's partner actually finds interesting. In general, veto power over a partner's relationships sounds safe but works terribly in practice and should be avoided. The rules may otherwise be set up in sneaky ways that will allow one person to date while, in effect, preventing others from doing so. Sometimes the manipulation is not explicit but emotional, even unconscious. I have seen situations where one person would always have a crisis at just the right time to keep their partner from going out on a date.

Manipulation is poisonous both to relationships and to casual connections. It is immoral and often abusive, and it's a terrible nonmonogamous strategy that will only bring you pain and drama. Let go of any urge to control partners' agency and relationships.

Difficult relationship structures.

I should mention another common difficult structure, namely closed ("polyfidelitous") triads and quads. Triads are three-person relationships where everyone is involved with each other to some degree, not necessarily sexually or romantically. Quads are the same for four people. People new to nonmonogamy are often attracted to closed triads and quads because they seem very similar to monogamy, and therefore safe. But this safety is usually an illusion. It is possible to have a happy, successful triad or quad, but these are advanced polyamorous structures that are pretty hard to pull off. They are relatively rare in nonmonogamous communities, and this is because they are difficult.

Most successful triads and quads seem to be open to their members dating outside the group. If you have a fantasy of a small closed group, I strongly recommend that you first spend time doing independent-dating forms of nonmonogamy. That means each person chooses their own partners and dates them separately. For most people, independent dating is easier and more sustainable. If you eventually form a triad or quad, the experience gained by dating independently will be highly valuable in making this structure work.

One common fantasy pattern is a couple (usually a straight man and a bisexual woman) looking for a third partner (usually a bisexual woman) to form a closed triad. This combines several bad elements: a closed small group, a one penis policy, and an unequal power dynamic between the pre-existing couple and the new woman. These hunting couples have a bad reputation as "unicorn hunters." Because of the difficult elements involved, either these couples fail to find a willing woman, the triad breaks up quickly, or longer-lived relationships devolve into bad power dynamics and resentment. I have seen men idealize this fantasy and get stuck in a pattern of failed searches for a decade or longer. Look instead for more realistic and balanced scenarios.

People new to nonmonogamy often focus on fulfilling their personal fantasies. But what makes nonmonogamy actually work is *getting used to your partners seeing other people*. Being able to do this makes you successful at nonmonogamy; not being able to do it means you will fail. The sooner you accept this reality, the sooner you will find your way to positive and comfortable nonmonogamous situations that fulfill you.

AUTHENTICITY AND INTEGRITY

A myth at the core of mainstream monogamous culture is that once we have the right partner, that person will satisfy us in every way and we will not want anyone else, whether for romance, sex, hobbies, or what have you. This almost never actually happens. Healthy people in healthy relationships, monogamous or not, have interests and connections outside the relationship. This was assumed in our great-grandparents' day when men and women had largely separate social spheres. But somehow modern romance lost track of the need for outside connection. Instead, our culture idealizes relationships where couples isolate themselves with "togetherness," depend only on each other, and cut other people out of their lives.

This myth includes the idea that when you get involved with one person sexually, you suddenly lose interest in anyone else. While this is true for some people, most of the population still gets interested in others from time to time. The myth requires denying or hiding these feelings, and probably lying about them to the person you are involved with. In order to maintain the wall that modern monogamy tries to build between couples and the outside world, it is generally necessary to engage in deception of self or others.

To be sure, most healthy monogamous people get over this in time and learn to accept their own sparks of interest and those of their partner. But most of us start with deception as a basic aspect of how we approach relationships. This is why infidelity is epidemic in monogamy. I consider cheating to be *part and parcel of the monogamous paradigm*, though it's disavowed as a violation of it.

This tendency towards deception and infidelity often stays with us as we move into our nonmonogamous journey. Which is to say, our first impulse is to hide what is happening, and to hide our partners from each other. Even folks who have made solid nonmonogamous agreements with each other tend to be wary about sharing details. A lot of people even start their nonmonogamous practice with an agreement to hide everything from each other, known as a "don't ask don't tell" agreement. These have a terrible reputation for brewing problems.

Men seem to be particularly susceptible to this urge to hide. In my experience, men are more likely than women to see truth as something that can be bent or simply denied. This is a generality—it is certainly possible to find women who constantly lie and men who are one hundred percent honest. But overall, men seem to be somewhat more likely to turn to deception as a default.

However, deceit is poison to any relationship, and triply so in nonmonogamy, where we do not have the support of the enclosing culture. In nonmonogamy we must negotiate our way to expectations and agreements—honestly and in good faith. The urge to hide anything from ourselves and our partners tends to scuttle most kinds of nonmonogamy. If people feel they cannot trust each other, connections are short-lived and fraught rather than strong and supported.

So, in order to be successful at nonmonogamy we need to learn to be authentic and have integrity, especially when it comes to sharing information about our lovers. This might sound easy in theory, but I cannot emphasize enough how hard it is in practice. Integrity has certainly been a lifelong journey for me. But at the end of the day, learning to just put everything on the table ends up feeling a lot safer, more rewarding, and all-around easier than deceit or omission.

TELLING AND HEARING THE TRUTH

The first part of integrity is of course just telling the truth. This is harder than it sounds. There's an ever-present temptation to minimize, omit important details, or tell supposedly harmless lies. A good question to always keep in mind is, would this person want to know the fact I am thinking about? If the answer is yes, it is important to tell them. Even if the truth is going to be hard to hear, even if it might start an argument. Never think you are protecting someone by being dishonest with them.

Some of my partners and I have identified what we call "that cheating feeling," that is, the urge to not say a hard truth and instead just let it slide. We have even come up with a ritual around it, where one of us will say, "I'm getting that cheating feeling." This signals to the other person that a hard truth is about to come out, and it is time to try to be open, understanding, and forgiving when hearing it.

This brings up an important point: truth-telling and truth-hearing is a two-way street. Being receptive to hard truths makes it much easier for people to tell them. The most honest relationships I have been in have been where both partners were open to hearing hard truths while reserving immediate judgment and avoiding quick emotional reactions. The primary responsibility for truth-telling lies in the person who needs to speak the truth, of course. But the skill of truth-*hearing* is equally important. If you blow up, get dismissive, or turn defensive when someone tells you a hard truth, they will stop telling you things.

I encourage you to practice truth-telling and truth-hearing regularly; these are skills that can be developed. This can be in the form of regular relationship check-ins, on the therapist's couch, or in other forms that work for you and your partners. You can even set up practice sessions where the truths being spoken are not about important matters at all.

TALKING ABOUT EMOTIONS

It is sometimes hard to say important things, because it can mean showing vulnerability. Still, it is very important to share what is emotionally real for us in a gentle but direct manner. This again is a skill that can be learned. Some of that is learning to identify what we are feeling, and some of that is learning to communicate it. Practice makes it easier.

Communicating emotions is sometimes tricky because of the impulse—by both you and the listener—to try to fix things immediately when emotions are difficult. But stay away from attempted solutions at first. Let the emotions happen and handle them as best you can. Sometimes feelings are fleeting, and will go away on their own. Sometimes emotions are deep-seated, rooted in childhood and triggered by the current situation.

It is important to understand that emotions are not truly *about* something; they are kind of their *own thing*. They do have a logic, but it is not the rationalist logic of the everyday world. They do not necessarily make sense, and may not be controllable. Nor do they necessarily require action. The action that helps an emotion may not be the one that logically makes sense. It is important to embrace and feel our feelings, in all their illogical glory, because actually *feeling them* is how we handle them, get through them, and learn to master them.

Talking about our emotions can be particularly difficult for men raised on the myth that showing emotions somehow makes us weak and unmasculine. The myth has it exactly wrong, of course—being vulnerable enough to describe one's emotions requires character and strength. To build good connections with people, it is important to recognize and lay out our emotional states, rather than just reacting to them in opaque and confusing ways.

Sometimes this may be extremely difficult—for example, if you are losing interest in a relationship. Still, walling off emotions always tends towards disconnection, and sharing one's feelings always tends towards connection.

It is important to speak truths, emotional or otherwise, with compassion. Some people use truth-speaking as a bludgeon. Instead, we should always consider the current context when speaking hard truths. If you are having negative thoughts about someone right now, but you are also very hungry or maybe frustrated by something at work, then perhaps you do not need to speak your thoughts until you have eaten or recovered. Keep your intent and your current emotional state in mind when speaking your truths. The goal of opening up with a lover is to be authentic, which then builds a closer connection. If you are using truth-speaking as a tool of manipulation or aggression, then that is not true authenticity.

Authenticity and integrity are especially important for nonmonogamy because we are not following the relationship rule book laid out for us by the culture. What we build, we have to build ourselves. Building new ways of connecting requires laying oneself on the line for one's lovers and partners to see.

Let's look at some common ways that authenticity shows up in nonmonogamy.

45

COMPARTMENTALIZATION

One way we are taught to be inauthentic is compartmental-ization: dating people very separately, rarely having them meet, and hiding details about each connection from the others. This model comes from monogamous expectations. Compartmentalization is how people have affairs, and how most people date between serious relationships. We expect that introducing our lovers or being honest with each person about the others will create disaster. In a monogamous scene, it very well may. Most of us have experienced trau-matic drama of this sort.

But in the nonmonogamy world, the opposite is true: being open about the important things in your life clears problems away, or prevents them in the first place. It takes a lot of experience in successful nonmonogamy to learn to trust in that truth.

I see a lot of men dragged down by their compart-mentalized dating practice, going on a handful of dates with one woman, a handful of dates with another, and ending up frustrated when they fail to build any deep or lasting connections.

Strong connections are built on trust and at least a minimal amount of social integration. In nonmonogamy, that means giving up on having one's connections remain entirely separate. Instead, find ways to bring people important to you together. At the most basic level, this means being up front and honest with each person about whom you are seeing. Be clear about what each person means to you, without downplaying, and avoid detrimental comparisons.

A near-universal nonmonogamous axiom is that having one's connections meet each other and get comfortable leads to more strength in those connections over the long term. It builds trust if your lovers can talk to each other. They can see that you are not telling one person one thing and the other something else. It also makes everyone feel more human and tends to defuse jealousy. A developed sense of empathy with other people in your dating network is crucial to your nonmonogamous success.

AVAILABILITY

Another piece of nonmonogamous authenticity is having good conversations about your availability. By that I mean what level of time and attention we expect to have available to each connection, with statements like "I'd like to see you once a month," or "caring for my child comes ahead of any lovers right now," or "I would like to see you socially more often," or "I want to stick to nonsexual touch with you."

Again, the monogamous world makes this kind of honesty difficult, even taboo. In monogamy, we are always supposed to be one hundred percent available to our one partner. Whether this is ever reasonable at all, it's certainly not in nonmonogamy. On top of that, I think that men have been trained by culture to think women are trying to trap us into marriage. Nonmonogamous women usually aren't, and they often have availability limits that supersede ours. This is another thing to get comfortable with. Boundaries are good, healthy, and necessary, and all parties should be able to set them.

Indeed, an inability to set or respect boundaries can quickly lead to disaster. Sometimes this happens because a connection grew past the limits of one partner, perhaps because they failed to *state* their limits. Or it could happen because someone felt unable to say no, and ditched out for self-protection. Having good boundaries is crucial, along with paying attention to the boundaries of the people you are with. And understand that boundaries may change and need to be redefined.

The need for the "availability discussion" has been a particularly hard lesson for me to learn. I have often been scared of telling a woman that I had some limit on my availability. But once I started opening up and actually having those conversations, I quickly discovered that the women I was dealing with were on the same page.

The other side of availability is also difficult. It can be hard to trust that a person really likes you if they are only available every other Friday. But nonmonogamous people are often especially busy. If someone wants to spend *any* of their time with you, that means they're interested in you. You can always ask for more connection, but you should be open to hearing a no. Never try to pressure or coerce someone into giving you more attention than they are willing to provide. Try to enjoy the positives you are getting rather than being miserable about what might be missing when measured by monogamous standards.

WOMEN AND AUTHENTICITY

Your authenticity means a lot to nonmonogamous women who date men. Women tell me endless stories about guys who lied about their other partnerships, were deceptive about their availability, couldn't manage to talk about their feelings, and so on. Women are so sick of this. They're sick of having to pressure guys to get honesty out of them. As a result, many will just bail at the first sign of deceit, dissembling, or omission.

It is pretty sad how low the bar has been set. The silver lining is that it's pretty easy to stand out from the crowd. The more authentic you become, the better life becomes for you and everyone around you.

WORKING ON OUR ATTRACTION TO WOMEN

Our culture raises us to believe a nasty myth: that women need to do a lot of work to be attractive, and men do not. Women are held to a highly idealized set of physical beauty standards, often unattainable, which privilege women who are thin, white, and highly feminine. Unlike women, men featured in the media are often considered attractive for their personality or accomplishments or just because they are men.

These attractiveness myths cause incalculable damage when it comes to dating, relationships, and hookups. So let's break down these myths and work with the nature of desirability. What qualities are you *actually* attracted to, as opposed to those you think you're *supposed to be* attracted to? How can we break with culture and discover or learn attractions that better fit our lives? How can we address our own attractive and unattractive qualities? How can we make changes so others find us more attractive? How can we stop trying to connect with women who are poor matches for us just because they fit the cultural beauty standard, and instead focus on women who are great matches for us?

CULTURAL DICTATES VERSUS ACTUAL DESIRES

As men, most of us have internalized the message that women's attractiveness is based on their bodies and that most of the women around us don't really qualify as attractive. And yet human sexuality is surprisingly contrary and resistant to cultural meddling. Our *actual* attractions will often contradict cultural standards, both in terms of physical and personality features. Indeed, personality and other nonphysical characteristics often govern attraction much more than looks or shape.

This disparity between our culturally dictated and actual attractions leads men into a weird double-think. We think we should be drawn to women who look a certain way, but we find ourselves often attracted to other women— sometimes consistently so. And we are often blind to this difference between theory and practice.

I have known many men who embodied this paradox—who would say they went for certain sorts of women (say, thin) but consistently dated others (say, heavy). This would happen across various axes: old versus young, tall versus short, quiet versus witty, and so on. Not only were these men harming themselves by being clueless about their actual interests, they would often end up shaming the women they were with. Such put-downs harm women and ruin otherwise compatible relationships.

This cultural focus on women's bodies distracts men from what is usually the most important part of attraction. Most men I have known, myself included, really dig particular personality types and cannot work with others. And yet it can take a long time to figure out what these personality types are because the dominant culture is so focused on bodies. Even with personalities, we are often confused by cultural stereotyping. For example, a guy might think he wants women with submissive personalities when he actually connects best with women who are strong-willed.

A third attraction, beyond body type and personality, is sensual and sexual chemistry. I consider this to be primarily a matter of personality matches. While sexual attraction certainly involves physical attraction, how sex (or non-sex sensuality) actually proceeds is a matter of what the people find interesting. There are many different ways to be sexual or sensual: gentle, rough, clean, dirty, transcendental, profane, highly connected, disconnected, carnal, platonic, voyeuristic, controlling, cooperative, calm, intense, etc. As in this list of examples, particular sensual modes can be compatible or completely incompatible. And of course there are particular sex acts that people prefer or dislike: oral, manual, sadomasochism, intercourse, restraint, butt play, same-room masturbation, and so on. It is important to find good or at least workable matches, as we will discuss in the section on consent.

While men are taught to feel physical chemistry, we are not taught to pay attention to nonphysical chemistry.

Commonly, a man will do the work to get in bed with a woman just because she is conventionally hot and assume that he'll figure out whatever sexual moves are needed once he gets her there. This is a recipe for bedroom disasters. Learning to identify your own sensual modes and attractions, and then learning to filter partners based on those, will lead to better encounters.

So spend the effort to figure out who you are actually attracted to and why. Do not waste your time chasing the women you think you *should* be attracted to, but instead focus on women you are *actually* compatible with. Men are not raised to be discerning, and we must learn to be discerning in this way.

EXPLORING OUR ATTRACTIONS

It is important to stay flexible and experiment in order to figure out your attractions. Still, we should do so in ways that treat women as people first and sex objects or relationship targets later. I see a lot of men who focus only on women they think fit their attraction profile—often conventionally attractive women—and pay attention only to these women when in social spaces or on dating sites. Instead, talk to everyone in a social space: women, men, and people of nonbinary genders, to practice treating people as people first.

Paying attention to a wide range of people in a social space may lead you to experimentation. You may suddenly find yourself attracted to or interested in someone you would not have approached if you were only looking from across the room. This moment of surprise attraction is very important, because it points out a place where our self-concept of who we're attracted to is incomplete. I have occasionally found myself in situations where someone seemed suddenly and inexplicably hot, and those occasions have brought deeper self-knowledge when I took the time to figure out what was going on. Nonmonogamy gives us a great opportunity to experiment.

Similarly, we often run into surprises in the bedroom. If someone clicked particularly well for us sensually, or if sex just did not work, do some introspection and think through what happened. Maybe it was a particular act or some dynamic between you and them. Focusing on how things felt from moment to moment will often alert you to exactly what is going on.

Beyond dating and sensuality, it is important to pay attention to long-term compatibility—that is, if you are interested in having long-term connections, whether deep or lightweight. I see a lot of men who consistently lose interest, sexual or otherwise, in partners at either the six-month or two-year mark. Some of these men may only find value in that special feeling that new relationships bring, but I think it usually happens because these men have not figured out what compatibilities are important to them long term. If you want stable longterm connections of any sort, pay attention to what aspects of a lover work for you not just when things are new, but also when the newness has worn off.

BREAKING WITH STEREOTYPICAL ATTRACTIONS

So far I have treated attraction as an internal quality, intrinsic and unchangeable. But our attractions are also a product of our environment and culture. This means they can change, often in a purposeful manner. I think we like to imagine our attractions as somehow mysterious and unchangeable because that removes our responsibility for them. It can feel scary to take responsibility for the effects our particular attractions may have, or to take on the task of making them less problematic.

I've talked about how who and what you find appealing is often contrary to cultural norms—attractions do seem to be a particularly ingrained aspect of people's personalities. However, people do tend to be attracted to what they are exposed to. If someone simply watches a lot of TV through their childhood, that may be enough to focus their attraction only on the types of women featured on TV.

Thinking about how we've been shaped by such influences, and what problems this might create for us and the women around us, is very scary. But it is important to face those hard truths about ourselves and see what we can do about them, in order to be better people and live better lives.

In particular, be wary when you are only attracted to women who are conventionally attractive in some way that corresponds with oppression, for example, women who are thin, highly feminine, or white. If you are consistently only attracted to women in one or more of these categories, you have probably somehow internalized the cultural indoctrination about desirability. Identifying this pattern allows you to work on it, either by discovering your other attractions or by retraining yourself to be more flexible. This can help you relate more authentically to women as people rather than as a series of culturally dictated desirability stereotypes.

Younger women.

Age is a difficult issue to consider in relation to attraction. Our culture gives us the very strong message that men, especially privileged or wealthy men, are entitled to date much younger women and fetishizes the bodies of younger women. I think mainstream porn increases this by providing images of very young women for fetishization or sexuality training. This is a kind of male entitlement and toxic for everyone. I see a lot of men (including progressive nonmonogamous men) internalize this age preference and defend this entitlement as something they have no control over and no responsibility for. If you are a man who consistently dates only younger women, then this is a piece of entitlement you should let go of.

The men I have met who only dated much younger women did so because of toxic attitudes they were carrying. Those attitudes consistently hurt the women and messed up their dating lives. Often men who date younger women are looking to control them—and remember that controlling behavior is a recipe for abuse. In some cases these men were fetishizing younger bodies, but fetishization itself is damaging because it treats women as things rather than people. And of course placing such emphasis on youth is unsustainable in a relationship as people age.

If you have a history of dating younger women, then it is important to let go of these harmful attitudes and learn to date your own age or older. Older women usually have a lot going for them: a stronger sense of self, more sexual experience, more confidence, more resources, and more. Dating near one's own age is typically just a matter of...starting to date near one's own age. Identify women you find attractive (maybe experimenting a bit) and start trying it out. You will probably be pleasantly surprised. If you find that you have a limit where you are not attracted to women over a certain age, then it may be time to work on retraining your sexuality, as described below.

Racial fetishization.

Fetishizing race is another behavior that bears mentioning. I cannot tell you the number of white men I have seen only date Asian women (often younger women) who fervently defend this fetishization. These men have often bought into the damaging stereotype of the exotic submissive Asian woman, and in most cases their consistent pursuit of these women is really only showing that they carry a problematic attitude. If you are a white man who only dates a particular racial minority, I encourage you to do some serious self-interrogation about what assumptions underlie your exclusion of other dating partners. I am referencing white men specifically because of the privilege dynamics at play—men of color who only date women of color tend to do so for reasons related to shared experience rather than fetishization. Doing some self-work here can help you connect more deeply by relating to women's personalities in more realistic and non-fetishizing terms.

Trans women.

Attraction to trans women is another consideration, along with attraction to people who have nonbinary gender or are gender nonconforming. I know a lot of men attracted ·to women who dismiss these potential partners out of hand, and I know trans women and masculine women who have real trouble getting dates in nonmonogamous communities as a result. Trans women are women, and if you are attracted to women you will probably find some trans women attractive. Similarly, men who consider themselves fully heterosexual are often attracted to people of nonnormative genders. If you find yourself only willing to date cisgender people, that may be a sign that you have some homophobia or transphobia issues that you could work on.

If you do find yourself interested in people who are trans, nonbinary, or gender nonconforming, please be aware that they may have had a traumatic life when it comes to dating and sensuality and act accordingly. Read up on trans issues to be confident that you are treating them sensitively and with respect. Be cautious of fetishizing the bodies of trans women—this can be just as damaging as dismissing trans women out of hand.

RETRAINING OUR ATTRACTIONS

I have been discussing attraction as a mutable thing. It is probably much easier to modify your attractions than you may expect. Often retraining attraction is a matter of figuring out what stereotypes or other problematic attitudes might be underlying a particular attraction. Once a problematic attitude is identified, then you can work your way past it.

Other times a particular attraction or fetish seems deeply ingrained and unmovable. When this happens people often give up changing themselves, and just try to work with it as it stands. If it is possible to do so purposefully, considering and mitigating any harm your attraction may be causing, then this is not a bad thing—not every problematic attraction needs to be altered. Still, it is probably easier to expand your repertoire than you might think.

An attraction reconditioning program often involves removal of conventional images (turn off the TV!) and choosing a new focus of attention. If you are a visual porn kind of person, you may want expand your choice of pornography. Porn is extremely varied these days, so it is possible to find most body types and sexual dynamics, though unfortunately it still tends to come packaged with bad fetishization tropes (racism, transphobia, and so on). If you are more into written erotica or fantasy, try to imagine objects of fantasy that expand your attractions in the direction you want. Out in the world, try interacting with a wider range of people, and seeing in what ways little bits of attraction may surface for you. See if you can focus in on those little sparks and fan them into flames. Expanding our attractions is difficult but worthwhile, as it helps break us out of a world where only certain people are worthy of connection.

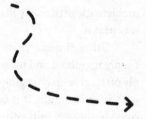

BEING ATTRACTIVE TO OTHERS

The other element of attraction to consider is women being attracted to us. As men, we have been well indoctrinated into the idea that *our* feelings of attraction are the ones that matter. The culture teaches men that any woman will fall for us if we do or say the right things. Or that women want alpha men, pickup artists, or whatever the latest take-your-money scam is trying to sell. These ideas are entirely wrong. Women are people with their own desires and agency, and so women will be attracted to you based on what traits they happen to like.

Accept that most women are simply not going to be attracted to you. People are just too varied for that. *The myth that any man can get any woman if he just works at it hard enough is a key piece of male entitlement.* It harms everyone, but especially women who are harassed and pursued when they are not interested. You need to separate this fantasy from the reality that only a fraction of women (probably a small fraction) will be attracted to you specifically, and therefore available.

MATCHING INSTEAD OF ATTRACTIVENESS

Reframe the challenge as *matching* with compatible people. You can improve your own attractiveness, and thus expand your dating pool, as we will discuss soon. But there is a danger in thinking that general (conventional) attractiveness is the answer. You cannot actually rank people's desirability on one linear scale. What women think is attractive varies widely from one to another.

If we focus on match compatibility, then our question is no longer "How can I be conventionally attractive?" and instead becomes "How can I attract the people I match best with?" To put it in deeper terms, "How can I either attract the people I am already a good match with, *or* become a person who matches well with the people I am interested in?"

Let's focus on that first part. How do we attract people we are well matched with? We find and accentuate the positive and interesting aspects of ourselves, whatever those might be. Perhaps you are an activist, or you have a certain interesting hobby, or you blog, or your work is interesting. Maybe you are really funny, or a great listener, or good at cooking fancy dinners. These are good qualities that set you apart. Think about how you might make them visible to the people around you. Maybe that means holding small events based on your hobby, or cooking dinners for a social group. Express the unique and exciting parts of your personality.

Sometimes our qualities or hobbies are particular sexual or kink skills, but these can be tricky to express. Putting "I really like to go down" on a personals site will likely actively turn women off—it sounds like the writer only values a woman for sex. Avoid erotic topics during initial contacts with women. It is usually best to save sexual compatibility matching for the third date or so.

MORE ATTRACTIVE, LESS UNATTRACTIVE

Let's talk about how we can healthily change ourselves to be more attractive. The central idea here is to be a better person, one whom other people will be more drawn to. There is a myth that women are attracted to guys who are mean or domineering. This is not true. Being better, in whatever way, is what makes you more attractive. The ways that work best for you will be particular to your personality and situation.

One way to change for the better is to find ways to just be nicer and more understanding. This is especially true if you build connections and understanding across subcultures or lines of oppression. If you build your understanding of people who are different from you—and of how the world is different for them—it opens up new possibilities for friendship and connection. They may be people of different sexualities, a different race, a different religion, and so on. Of course, you should not do this simply to get more dates—you should do it in order to be a better person. Still, doing this tends to open up a lot of dating possibilities that would otherwise be closed.

Beyond that, consider the traits that make us *unattractive*. Being funny is great, but if you advertise your humor by talking over everyone else, people won't like you.

Great sexual skills will not get anyone into your bed if you are habitually mean or self-centered. Men do commonly have personality traits or bad attitudes that make them largely un-datable. These men tend to have a blind spot, unable to see the real problem. When thinking about your attractiveness, think about your qualities that are not so great. You may already know what they are, but it is a good idea to check in with some honest friends who will give you real feedback. Listen to them as your guide in how to move forward with altering your personality or physicality. Often this can be simpler than you expect—a friend may just tell you that the jokes you make are not funny, and you can stop and that's it. Sometimes the changes are more significant. They might involve you reading up on subjects, getting a handle on deep emotional issues, or altering the way you live your life. But those changes are worthwhile whatever the dating outcome. Often our search to date better guides us to be better people in general, which opens new possibilities in various parts of our lives.

PHYSICAL ATTRACTIVENESS

Physical appearance is also something to think about. Whatever you look like, make an effort to show that you are presenting your look deliberately. If you don't think a man's appearance matters, or shouldn't matter, you are behind the times. Things are slowly changing in this regard, towards a more balanced future where men and women pay equal attention to their physical attractiveness. But we're not there yet, and a lot of guys still have major blind spots around their appearance.

I don't necessarily mean hitting the gym. A lot of guys confuse musculature or fitness with male attractiveness. Bodies are very hard to change, and trying too hard can harm us physically and mentally. In general it's a poor idea to try to be more attractive by adhering more closely to cultural norms, physical or otherwise. By and large, experience shows that it is better to change yourself to be *less* culturally normative, not more.

I am talking about accentuating parts of our appearance that are interesting or unique, that is, what we wear, the small things we do to our bodies, what tattoos we have or display, etc. Maybe you should display those tattoos, wear that activist T-shirt, put on some leather, or paint your eyebrows with glitter. A key to looking good is feeling good. Think about what appearance changes make you feel sexy and at home in your body. Maybe that means being hairy, maybe it means shaving everything. If wearing suits makes you feel sexy, wear suits, perhaps even in situations that do not call for dressing up. If wearing skirts makes you feel sexy, wear skirts. Experiment with your look and see what really speaks to you, and what speaks to people around you.

THE INEVITABILITY OF COMPATIBILITY

Thinking of attractiveness as *matching* another person's likes also does away with one of the biggest dating mistakes men make, which is focusing on their "approach." Forget the pickup lines. How you approach a woman does not matter that much, aside from showing some basic respect. Either you are a good match—which means that both you and she think so—or you are not. If you are, chances are you will get together sooner or later. If you are a bad match, it will either not happen or not last. There is a kind of inevitability about dating, and it is important to work with that inevitability and not obsess about any particular interaction. I have had a number of great relationships (and some sexual connections) start extremely awkwardly and haltingly. Turns out if we like each other, awkwardness and missteps are okay! If we don't, no amount of smooth-talking will help.

So figure out who matches really well with you, and make the effort to pursue or attract those people. Do not pester incompatible women—you are just forcing them to turn you down. Your history can be a very good clue: when you have dated women and it went well, what qualities did those women share? Focus on women with those qualities, and you will save a lot of time and get much better matches.

NONMONOGAMOUS COMMUNITY

The single biggest contributor to successful nonmonogamy is finding a nonmonogamous community and integrating into it. People who join a community of experienced, supportive fellow explorers usually succeed in their nonmonogamous journey. People who do not tend to fail.

This makes sense when we think about nonmonogamy as a set of skills. Mainstream culture expends a lot of effort training people how to do monogamy well. Nonmonogamy has its own set of skills, rituals, and learned lessons that are necessary for success, and these are different. Most of us come to nonmonogamy not having learned any of these skills. You can learn a certain amount from books. However, people acquire knowledge better and understand it more deeply when learned from other people: from role models, conversations, observation. So, meaningful learning about nonmonogamy requires having community with experienced people who are successful at it.

Also, as we have discussed, the process of getting into nonmonogamy can be emotionally fraught. Communities provide not just knowledge, but also support. That might mean leaning on a friend, sharing at a discussion group, or just talking to people who understand where you are coming from.

Further, a community can be your best dating pool. Getting nonmonogamy right is much easier when dating other people who are nonmonogamous and preferably experienced at it. One does not normally run into these people at the grocery checkout, at a bar, or at work. Instead they must be sought, and the easiest way to find nonmonogamous people is by entering one or more nonmonogamous communities.

They take different forms. Online discussion groups offer advice, friendship, and encouragement. You can also find forums at swinging and BDSM (kink) dating websites. There are in-person swinging and sex-party communities, where folks might meet for social events with a sexual flair. Polyamorous communities excel at setting up clothes-on discussions and social events: dinners, support groups, bar nights, potlucks, and conferences. And there are other communities that have a lot of nonmonogamous people in them, such as dance communities, queer communities, and gamer communities.

Women seem to seek out nonmonogamous community fairly readily, but many men avoid finding or joining communities. Two myths seem to promote this behavior. First, men are conditioned to be individualistic whatever the cost. Second, there is a general myth around relationships, and especially nonmonogamous connections, that they should just happen by magic, and not require any learning or skills. Because of these myths, many men think that the best way to be nonmonogamous is to do it in isolation.

I also think that there's a power thing going on—I suspect that some men are unwilling to enter communities because they believe they will have more choice if they are not held accountable to community norms. They think they can do nonmonogamy however feels right to them. But as we have discussed, what feels right and what actually works sustainably are two different things. Developing nonmonogamy on one's own mostly results in poorly informed choices with bad outcomes.

So, be good to yourself—do things the easy way. Find a community, preferably several communities, and engage with them. Approach them with curiosity and humility, looking to learn and adapt. Here you can find the skills, support, and potential dating partners you want.

SMALL COMMUNITIES

You may encounter some difficult aspects within these nonmonogamous communities. They are often hard to enter. Nonmonogamous people are typically closeted and concerned about exposure. Worse, they are used to fending off a constant stream of bad actors (usually men) who try to enter and commit harmful acts: nonconsensual touching, rude come-ons, or sexual assault. Nonmonogamous groups have usually built up defenses against such people. You will want to present your best self and impress people, and you will need to take the time to learn the habits and ways of a particular community. There are no shortcuts here. Often it takes months to really break into a particular social set or community, whether we're talking discussion-oriented dinners, sex parties, or other activities. We will discuss common social etiquette in a later section.

In addition, nonmonogamous communities are generally small. Even if you live in a major urban area, the people you're looking for probably number only in the tens of thousands. Which might sound like a lot, but it ends up feeling like a small town. Imagine you're driving into a town with a sign saying "population 10,000." You'd probably think of it as a small town, not a big city. You'd imagine that most people know each other, or know *of* each other, and everyone knows each other's business. That is what nonmonogamous communities are like: not very big, and word really gets around.

This means reputation is very important. You should aim to have a good reputation, not through trickery or by putting up a false front, but by just straight-up being a better person. A good reputation in a community means that more people will be interested in you, both as a friend and as a potential date or hookup. On the other hand, screwing up in a major way will swiftly get you a bad reputation. This can happen if you fail at basic integrity, act nasty towards an ex, try to set up a double-standard situation, and so on. A bad reputation will make women pass you by, and social invites will dry up.

If folks seem to be avoiding you, or you are uninvited from nonmonogamous events, it is time to check your behavior. You are probably doing something that is turning people off. If you can, get honest feedback on what is happening. Listen to this feedback and improve your behavior surrounding whatever issues you have. It can be tempting to dismiss people's concerns as nonsense, or to blame your issues on gossip or drama, but getting defensive will just dig you into a deeper hole, because what you are really saying is that you are unwilling to be accountable for your own actions. Whatever the issue is, being a better person will solve it and nothing else will. Again, there are no shortcuts.

THE GENDER RATIO

Due to the way our culture encourages nonmonogamy in men and discourages it in women, more men are interested in nonmonogamy. Not many more, but enough to skew the dating pool. In any particular community, the ratio might vary from about even to somewhat more men (say, up to fifteen percent more). That's not a lot of difference, but one can definitely feel it in the dating market.

Also, for lightweight connections such as hookups, men are socialized to be more interested in them than women. So women who want them can have an easier time finding them. However, when it comes to dating connections, the gender difference tends to disappear. And it reverses for other sorts of arrangements, like co-parenting.

I know plenty of nonmonogamous women who cannot seem to make the connections they are looking for and are very frustrated about this.

The upshot is that nonmonogamous women (who are attracted to men) are more in demand than monogamous women, and they know it. Beyond that, nonmonogamous women are typically liberal and feminist, so they are less likely to put up with crap. They tend to be empowered in relationships, more comfortable in their bodies, more confident in their sexuality, and more likely to be queer. Which are great things! But it means that the men who date them need to rise to the occasion. I frequently see men retain a lot of bad and disrespectful habits from their monogamous dating experiences, where such habits may have been workable. Treating women disrespectfully in any way will not work well for you in nonmonogamy.

A factor that eases the gender imbalance is that nonmonogamy itself tends to absorb number differences. This is because nonmonogamy is not the scarcity economy of monogamy—most nonmonogamous people are at least somewhat available. So if there's a ten percent gender difference, it may simply mean that women who date men get ten percent more dates. Not a big difference. The dating pool can stretch and accommodate, so almost everyone is able to form connections.

I see a lot of men descend into bitterness regardless. I think they are stuck in the scarcity mentality of highly competitive monogamous dating scenes. These men get obsessed with gender ratios at any particular event—they will whine about it and refuse to return. They go on endless quests to find some mythical dating venue where women outnumber men, but those do not actually exist. Men who have gone down this spiral of negativity *make themselves super unattractive*, coming across as entitled whiners who are used to being catered to, and who are surprised when they are no longer in a privileged situation.

Do not be one of those guys. If you are having trouble dating in a nonmonogamous scene, that means it is time to adapt and redouble your efforts. Do what you need in order to show up, stand out, and be your best self. Do not be discouraged at events that are more than fifty percent men: community-entry events and dating events tend to have a skewed ratio and do not reflect the entire community. Instead, learn to trust in the abundance that comes with nonmonogamy. Take the time to really dig into communities and get to know people. The more you do, the more dating options become available.

SOCIALIZING AND FLIRTING

Socializing while nonmonogamous is different from socializing while monogamous, and the differences can mess up someone new to the scene. Mainstream social circles tend to be very couple-centric, but nonmonogamous people are not really categorized as "single" or "coupled." Therefore, social scripts based on those categories no longer apply.

For instance, nonmonogamous people are usually more available for dating and more open to casual touch and cuddling—but flirting and negotiating touch are therefore different and more focused on *consent*. Further, it is common to socialize with one's lovers' lovers, along with exes, and nonmonogamous people have created new social expectations to handle these situations. This can all feel challenging at first, but with time people settle in and get comfortable socializing like they always have—just with more touching, more direct discussions, more possibility, and more complex connections.

As mentioned, nonmonogamous communities tend to be wary of outsiders. This is for good reasons: keeping out aggressive men, and keeping community members safe from exposure that could cost them their jobs, friends, or family. There are purposefully set obstacles to getting in, and that's actually a sign of a healthy community. The key here is to take it slow. Take your time, be polite and friendly, really engage with people, and treat them as interesting individuals. It is a good idea to hold off on hitting on people until you have gotten to know a group fairly well and have been accepted by them. Your goal is to get comfortable, get to know people, and let people get to know you. This will take some time—usually multiple events across multiple months.

RESPECTING WOMEN SOCIALLY

There is another level of distrust we should discuss, the distrust that women often have around men. To paraphrase a known saying, when a man goes out on a first date with a woman, he worries about being embarrassed or rejected. When a woman goes out on a first date with a man, she worries about being raped or murdered. Moreover, a man who harms women will typically have some protection in his culture and social group and be believed ahead of the survivor. This is part of rape culture. Women who experience harm at the hands of men typically have little recourse or justice. Sexual harassment reminds women of this fairly often.

Nonmonogamous women are seen as particularly unprotected targets for harassment and abuse. Most have had their boundaries ignored or devalued by the culture and by individual men. So, women in nonmonogamous circles will often be on their guard, especially around men they do not know. You should respect this fear, which is legitimate, and be respectful and careful in your social interactions with nonmonogamous women. Consent is a major piece of this respect and care and we will talk about it later in this section.

One way to show respect towards women is by engaging with everyone at a social event. Your goals when socializing should be getting to know people and having a good time, rather than getting laid or picking someone up. This is true of any nonmonogamous gathering, even sex parties. Try to step outside your usual zone and talk to people you would not normally engage with, including men. Making connections with people of all genders will be how you integrate with a group. Be interested in people's whole lives—things like their jobs and what they do for fun. Do not be one of those guys who enters a room and makes a beeline for attractive women. This is objectifying behavior, which women will notice and avoid.

You may find it uncomfortable to chat with people who are already lovers of women you are interested in, but try to get past that discomfort and connect with these folks. It is important to embrace the awkwardness and dive in. In these circles, engaging with a person's partners is *part of getting to know them*. And it's a crucial part of acknowledging them as a nonmonogamous person with agency. Really, this is a standard nonmonogamy test. If you can be happy and comfortable around a woman's lovers, you show that you have a handle on your jealousy and are not carrying much monogamous baggage. Generally, refusing to talk to someone's partners is a big turnoff and will lead people to avoid you.

EXTENDED CONSENT

An important social ritual of nonmonogamous spaces is what I think of as extended consent, that is, the extension of sexual consent practices out into the social arena. The most obvious place this shows up is touching. Nonmonogamous people tend to be much more explicit in their conversations around any kind of touch, including casual social touch. I live in California, which is pretty much the hugging capital of the world, but even here people have been asking for permission before every hug, using "Hug?" shorthand questions. The same goes for things like touching someone's shoulder or knees. As with any consent request, cheerfully hear a no and thank the person for taking care of their boundaries.

Beyond touching, though, get in the habit of extended consent around social practices themselves. If you are considering joining a conversation that people are already in, try saying something like "You seem to be pretty engaged with each other—is it okay if I join you?" When talking with women, or anyone really, you should give them an occasional chance to leave, to make sure they still want to be in the conversation with you. Perhaps say something like "I'm enjoying this conversation, but I don't want to keep you. We can stop talking anytime you want." In general, whenever a social situation seems like it might be awkward or going oddly, try saying something about this! It turns out that people usually appreciate this explicit meta-conversation, and checking in will often defuse a situation that is feeling weird in some way.

Extended consent is important because it helps everyone in a social situation exercise their agency. Beyond that, if you engage in extended consent it signals to the women around you that you care about their boundaries and will act with respect.

OBJECTIFICATION

While socializing, any objectifying language will be a turn-off. Objectification means treating a person like a thing, especially a thing for your own consumption. There are a lot of verbal ways that men may indicate that they think of women as objects. In nonmonogamous community this is especially an issue, because people tend to be more available and flirty, and sex is usually in the air. Guys sometimes respond to this atmosphere by ratcheting up the objectification, which ironically makes most women avoid them.

So, while flirting, don't compliment a woman's body parts. Complimenting something she *had choice over* is much better, like her outfit or hairstyle. But even better, think about what made her attractive to you in the moment. If it is just her looks, you may not actually be attracted to her once you talk to her. Try talking to her, and if you are still attracted, her personality is also part of what is attracting you. Compliment her personality or say good things about the discussion. In general, you should be speaking to women's personalities, even (especially!) women you are physically attracted to.

Similarly, don't use the word "female" to refer to a woman or women. These are people, not muskrats on a nature hike. Other words that are diminishing or sexualizing should also be stricken from your vocabulary: "hottie," "miss," "babe," and so on.

Objectification often intersects with the fetishization we discussed earlier. You might think you are being open-minded, but if you compliment a woman on some aspect of herself that marks her as part of a marginalized group or an oppressed class, that produces a double dose of yuckiness for her. She is being both objectified and reduced to a fetish at once. For example, telling a woman of color that you find the shade of her skin beautiful will turn her off quickly. Telling a large woman that you like her cleavage will likely lose you that date. Talking to a physically disabled woman about your medical fetish will cause her to exit the conversation so fast your head will spin.

None of this means you should avoid *having* physical attractions. There comes a time to engage with physicality, and that is usually once you are in the bedroom doing sexual or sensual things. The social world is not the place for this focus. There is an art to feeling physical attraction as it happens, and noting it, and letting it go so it doesn't dictate the interaction. There is no need to be in a hurry—you will see these people again in the small communities we are talking about.

Avoid staring. Really, do not look at women for very long unless you are actually talking to them, because staring is a clear sign to them that you are objectifying. Nor should you mentally indulge in sexual fantasies about the people you see. Staring and fantasizing are creepy. Avoiding staring will help you refocus on nonvisual, nonphysical aspects of women.

FLIRTING AND GETTING DATES

Let's say you notice a woman who seems interesting. What next? If you are not already in a conversation with her, do not upend the social order to get into one. Do not make a beeline for her, or interrupt an intense conversation she might be in. And don't try to talk to a woman who is alone and giving off "Don't talk to me" signs, like looking at her phone or resting in a corner. Be patient and wait for the natural flow of socializing to bring you together. Or just keep an eye out for opportunities—if she ends up in a conversation with someone you already know, maybe take the chance to join them (with consent!). If it doesn't happen at this event? You'll probably run into her again.

Once in a conversation with a woman you are attracted to, talk and have a good time! Avoid cornering her. Do not ignore others in the conversation either. Look for signs she might be interested in you as well, such as a lot of focus on you, interest in what you are saying, flirty or sexy comments, and the like. You are engaging in a dance of sorts, where you and she take turns expressing interest and noting the interest of the other—if it is there. Give her chances to take her turn at expressing interest and wait for her to come to you. You can even literally wait for her to come to you—end the conversation after a while and see if she comes and finds you later. But also give her turns in intensifying the flirting—if you say something flirty, let it go and see if she returns with something flirtatious later in the conversation. If she does not come back to you or return a flirtation, then she is probably not interested.

There is that point where interest seems to be happening on both sides, but neither has taken the step of making that interest clear. In the past, the next step would be one party (usually a man) giving the other their phone number or asking for a number. That is pretty obsolete in this day and age, and I recommend against it. Phone numbers feel really aggressive now that we have other ways of getting in contact. Social media is the current favored technique. If you like someone at an in-person event, probably the best way to make your interest clear is to find them on a social network after the event (because you are probably socially connected in some way) and send them a nice note. Something short and vague like, "I really enjoyed our conversation yesterday—thank you! I would be delighted to talk more if that interests you." Or, wait for *her* to send *you* a nice note.

Never pressure a woman for a date. If a woman says no, thank her and stop pursuing her or talking to her. If a woman does not write back or return interest in some obvious way, let it drop and give her some extra space in social situations for a while. *You are never entitled to a woman's attention or to a date. Let go of any idea that a woman will start to like you if you just put in the effort.* Being rejected or ignored is a gift, because it saves you the time and trouble of pursuing a connection that is not going to work.

SOCIALIZING WITH PARTNERS OF PARTNERS

Once you are actually dating one or more people, there is the additional issue of learning to socialize with your partners' partners in the room. Dealing with a romantic interest's other lovers is downright weird at first. The monogamous culture does not give us any tools for this and even insists that everyone should be upset about the situation. Learning to be comfortable with people in your dating network is crucial to successful nonmonogamy. People entering nonmonogamy often assume that everyone will stay separate and no one will meet, but that tends to be unworkable. Or they assume that everybody will be fast polyamorous friends just because they date the same people, but that's usually too much to assume. Nonmonogamous social situations can be difficult—socializing is a prime source of jealousy, competitiveness, and feelings of abandonment, and social blowups can damage a nonmonogamous network. On the other side, good practices help to relax everyone and let them humanize each other.

So get away from awkwardness and settle into treating everyone normally. Things will probably be awkward at first. Use techniques like explicitly acknowledging the awkwardness ("I know this is kind of weird, but I'd like to get to know you better") or just being extra friendly and outgoing.

At first, people socializing in these situations can get obsessed over each lover who is present getting the same amount of time and attention. It is important to relax about this—the randomness of socializing will prevent an entirely equal balance of attention. I prefer a model of acknowledgment, that is, acknowledge all of one's connections at an event. That might just mean a hug and a kiss, or it might mean some conversation, or it might mean being introduced as someone's partner. Not feeling acknowledged feels crappy, like you're some kind of dirty secret instead of a legitimate connection. Establish what basic acknowledgment looks like to each person, by talking to them about it in advance, and then follow through on that.

Making a plan before an event can help. Sometimes you may be on a date or otherwise focused on one person during an event, but plan ways to acknowledge other people you are connected to. Or you may wish to switch between connections as an event progresses, or perhaps socialize with multiple partners at once. Or if you're not on a date, you may want to spend most of your time talking to new people. All these possibilities can bring up hard emotions, so it is good practice to ask each person what they are looking for prior to the event, and negotiate a plan. Your plan can be vague, and it might be updated during the event as people's needs change, but having a plan is golden. It should include checking in with everyone you are close to during an event.

What about exes? Mainstream monogamous culture tells us to avoid exes, even if it means abandoning a whole social group. That's usually not possible in our small nonmonogamous communities. Indeed, your ex may date someone you are dating, or be otherwise involved in your dating network. In general, it is very important to stay on good terms with your exes (and former hookups) in non-monogamous community, and that also extends to social events. If you can, be friendly and acknowledge them as a person to whom you were once connected. If the breakup was bad or there is bitterness, try to be accommodating and give them space. This may extend to finding ways to avoid being at the same events as them. For any breakup, be considerate and try to avoid making out (or having sex at play parties) in front of recent exes. Be friendly or at least considerate, knowing that it takes time to get past a breakup.

These new rituals and situations can be especially difficult for introverts and people who feel socially awkward. Learning to be comfortable in this world may take some time and effort, but it yields huge rewards. Nonmonogamous communities are typically friendly, cozy, sexy, and highly connected. They tend to be hyper-social because of the extra layer of availability and connection. Once one is past the challenges, it's common to build an extensive and interwoven social network. This can bring us many things: a view into much wider human possibilities, abundant cuddling and other nonsexual touch, a support network that extends well beyond dating, and a constant stream of new people to meet.

NAVIGATING PLAY PARTIES

Erotic parties are a particularly challenging and interesting subculture. Most nonmonogamous people end up at least visiting these events at some point, but only some end up enjoying them and attending regularly. It takes time to get used to events where people take their clothes off and get it on. Sexy events are a particular kind of nonmonogamy that not everyone enjoys. Some people just aren't into exhibitionism or voyeurism.

The terms "sex party" and "play party" are used pretty interchangeably. They refer to events where it is acceptable to have sex and/or engage in BDSM play. Still, these are social events first and sexy venues only secondarily, much as they might be fired up with erotic energy. Usually the social and sexy areas will be separated. When attending these events, it's important to think about them as social venues first and foremost.

Play parties are probably not what you expect. They're not a giant pile of bodies. They are definitely not a sexual free-for-all. It is very rare to hook up with people you do not know. Most depictions of sex parties in popular media have it totally wrong, so people often come to them with some pretty incorrect ideas and expectations. Particular party scenes will have their own rules, rituals, and expectations. It is important to approach any play party scene with an open mind and few expectations.

MAKING IT TO THE PARTY

The first challenge of exploring a play party scene is just getting in the door. These events are never really public, due to the potential for poorly behaving men to show up and ruin things. Many play parties are private house parties among friends, and to be invited you will have to impress current attendees as being a good fit. Other events are semi-public but will have a series of obstacles to getting in—signing up for memberships, filling out forms, attending with established members, coming with partners, attending a workshop, and so forth. These obstacles are purposefully put in place to weed out men who are self-centered and think that sex parties are some kind of ticket to a quick lay. So, do not be such a man. You should cheerfully jump through whatever hoops it takes to join an event. If there is a form, fill it out in detail. If you are expected to learn lists of rules, do so, and follow them carefully. If volunteering to help at the party is an option, volunteer—it is a great way to meet people. Sexy events are typically ad hoc with a small budget, so they will appreciate help setting up and arranging refreshments and supplies.

Once you get into a scene, stay on your most respectful behavior. If a host or guest brings something up about your behavior, listen to them respectfully, apologize, and make changes as needed. These are private events where people are kicked out for rudeness or boundary violations all the time, and those bans are typically permanent. Being invited to sexy parties is a privilege reserved for those who contribute positively.

TOUCHING AND CONSENT

The first rule is no touching without consent. Because sexiness is in the air, everyone is paradoxically much more on their guard about touching than at your usual social event. So no touching without verbally asking, ever. This includes tapping someone on the shoulder, touching someone's hair, and so on. Keep your hands to yourself until you get a yes. This is doubly true for men—everyone is on their guard about guys acting badly, so there is little leeway for men to mess this up.

You will see some people walk through a room and touch pretty much everyone, or jump into a group on a mattress, or just walk up to folks and kiss them. It may look like a gropey free-for-fall, but what you are failing to see is that these particular people already know each other well. Be assured that they have had thorough consent discussions in the past. If you hang around and get to know people, you may someday be that person, but it will take time and good behavior to get there.

The separate area where people are getting it on usually has special rules: do not linger or stare, do not talk loudly or otherwise distract people, do not try to join in with people already engaged, and do not masturbate on your own while watching others unless they've explicitly told you it's okay. The expectation is that people set up any hookups while elsewhere in the social space, then enter the play space with their play partner(s) and a plan. Also, play parties will often have rules around safer sex, for instance, requiring condoms for all penetration.

If you are at a play event and someone violates your boundaries, or violates the boundaries of a person you are attending with, please report it to the hosts as soon as possible. If you are not in an emotional space to do so just yet, that's fine. But if you see someone else's boundary being violated, please report it, even if you were not involved in any way. Most people running sex or play events really want to know about boundary issues early so they can handle the situation right away. A person who disrespects somebody else's body once will probably do it again, often at the same event.

KEEPING YOUR EXPECTATIONS LOW

The main challenge of sex parties is managing your expectations. A sex party can be an intense place, full of erotic possibilities, and it is very easy to get overwhelmed with all the things that could theoretically happen. However, letting your expectations get out of control will put you in a counterproductive emotional state: feeling desperate and overstimulated. People in this state tend to hit on people inappropriately. Or they might crash emotionally when they realize the night's fantasies are not coming true. Keep your expectations low and your head together.

At sex parties, people almost always get it on with people they already know and like. And people go through the full negotiations necessary for sex to happen. This also applies to other erotic activities that may happen at these events, like massages or kink play. Everything in the previous section on socializing applies—sex parties are just another social venue. Take your time, get to know the community, be friendly, and meet people. Focus on socializing rather than hooking up.

I strongly recommend going to your first play party with a plan to not engage in any sex or play at all. Instead just explore the venue and get comfortable being there. Any time you attend a sex party without one or more lovers, you should expect that nothing sexy will happen. If something does happen it will be a pleasant surprise, and if nothing happens you avoid disappointment. Thinking of an event as primarily social will help reduce nervousness or anxiety, two challenging feelings that arise when entering the sexy party world.

ATTENDING WITH PARTNERS

The best way to make some play happen is to show up with a lover or lovers of your own, and a plan to play with them. Again, set up plans and expectations with partners in advance. Consult with your lover(s) about how you want to socialize and respond to any interest from other people. If you are attending with one lover on a date, should you spend all your time together, most of your time, or just some? Are you or they available for erotic interactions with others, and how much so? Is there a time in the evening you would like to rejoin each other and get down to some play?

Play parties are a rich and chaotic place, so be ready to adapt if your plans fall through. Sometimes people get overwhelmed or tired and need to leave. Or perhaps the play room fills up and there is nowhere to have sex. Plans will often go awry—that woman you wanted to engage with at midnight might end up in an encounter that does not end in time. It is important to put your ego aside along with any expectations, and roll with surprises that might come up. Avoid getting attached to any particular outcome at any particular party. These events are typically held regularly, and if this month did not work out to your satisfaction, just come back next month.

Even when you make it into the play room, you may find that sex itself is more difficult than usual. Sex in a room full of other people having sex is … different. It takes some getting used to. Some people find that they cannot focus on their partner or engage erotic energy. Men often have trouble with erections. Group sex scenes can develop weird dynamics. Kink play might face insufficient space for back-swings. There may be loud music, interruptions, or other challenges. It is important to take it easy and approach public sex or kink with a playful and noncommittal air. Just see what happens. The more you try things out at these events, the more relaxed you will be, and the more fun you will have.

On top of all this, there are special concerns around attending play parties with multiple partners. Seeing or hearing your partner engage erotically with someone else may challenge you. A lover of yours may suddenly start flirting or connecting with someone, catching you off-guard. Or the disappointment of a failed plan can be hard to take when your partners have other partners present. Overall, erotic events are a big potential trigger for any nonmonogamous issues that may be lurking under your covers. Even highly experienced nonmonogamous people sometimes consider play parties to be challenging and end up having difficult nights.

HOLDING IT TOGETHER

Keep a close eye on your emotional state and the emotional state of anyone with you at play parties. It is easy to slip into desperation, overstimulation, nervousness, disappointment, jealousy, or other anti-social emotions. Take care of yourself. This might mean taking breaks to decompress, sticking to the social area, having something to eat, whatever. However, be careful about turning to intoxication. Having too much to drink (or overdoing other substances) is a common problem at sex parties and often leads to people being thrown out. Some parties require sobriety for this reason.

I strongly recommend attending your early events sober and limiting your intoxication at later events. Also, it's a good idea to simply leave an event if you or anyone in your group seems to be losing it. I have a rule for myself that I just leave if I hit a certain level of overstimulation, frustration, tiredness, or social burnout. That rule has kept me from making a fool of myself more times than I can count. You can come back next time.

Of course, you may conclude that erotic events are not for you, and that's fine. These parties are really not for most people. Even among the highly experienced polyamorous people I know, only about half like to go to sex parties. Some might not be down for the emotions that arise, or they may simply not enjoy that kind of erotic energy.

Sexual events of this sort do, however, create an interwoven intimate community that is very special—one where people have many personal and erotic connections to others. It is hard to describe the comfort and abundance that is available in these communities. They are in many ways a different world—one very much worth exploring.

PAYING ATTENTION TO OUR CONNECTIONS

The one thing that seems to most set me apart from other nonmonogamous men is that I am consistently good at maintaining connections. Dates are sacred to me and I keep them reliably. Between dates, I put in the effort to stay connected by texting, calling, and socializing with my partners. Women frequently tell me how much they appreciate this. Because for some reason, many nonmonogamous men fail to *consistently respect the time and attention* of the women they are seeing.

Let's examine the art of giving attention. How can we consistently stay attentive to the women we see? How can we respect their time? How can we move past our fears of overcommitment and treat the women in our life better?

ATTENTIVE DATING

The obvious first step is to make dates and keep them. They can be as casual as "Hey, want to get together Friday?" or they can involve putting a date on the calendar months in the future. The key is to keep your word and show up. *Consistently*.

I've seen so many bad habits when it comes to keeping dates. There are guys who purposely overbook their nights and then pick a plan at the last minute. There are guys who never call women back but then booty-call them on Saturday night. There are the guys who seem to cancel *every* plan. Or they modify plans at the last minute to involve other people or less time. Women rarely go on second or third dates with these guys, and once word gets around the community, first dates also dry up.

The other big failing is staying connected between dates. Again, this should not be hard. Exchange the occasional text message, say hello at social events. I hear all the time from women that some lover did not text them back, ignored them at a party, failed to follow up on a plan, or something similar. When you ignore women, they usually assume you're either not attracted or doing something shady. And then they bail. So send a nice follow-up message a couple days after a date or other get-together. Check in if it has been a month since you last talked, even if your connection is only occasional. And for fuck's sake, when women contact you, call or message them back.

SOCIAL ACKNOWLEDGMENT

A similar issue is making your connection socially visible. Acknowledging your connections socially tends to solidify them. I give extra hugs and kisses to people I have recently dated. Maybe you just say hello or introduce them to your friends and partners, possibly saying something about how you are connected.

Sometimes people are cagey about social recognition because they have highly compartmentalized connections, or because they worry that simple social acknowledgment will somehow overcommit them. Move past these fears. Failing to acknowledge your lovers socially will definitely drive them away from you. Nobody likes feeling like someone's dirty secret or disposable action on the side. Decompartmentalizing your relationships will make you notably more available and attractive to nonmonogamous women.

MEN AND ATTENTIVENESS

There are of course some exceptions. I have run into a handful of women who would not make solid plans with me, and instead would booty-call me once in a while. Some women only wanted to meet at parties. But overall, there's a gender thing here, and it's men who tend to behave irresponsibly.

However, with the bar set so low, it's easy to stand out! Make promises and keep them. Show up when you say you will. Stay in contact and show up for conversations. Follow up with your partner's other lover when your partner asks you to. Consistently keeping small promises and following up on minor expectations will help people like you. Which is true in every part of life.

Why do so many nonmonogamous men have trouble with this? It's usually due to some psychological barrier we carry. I think that being inconsistent or hard to pin down is a way that guys try to prevent overcommitment. Men use these behaviors to signal non-commitment or limit connections. Again, this comes back to a fear of being tricked or railroaded into monogamy.

But nonmonogamous women are not actually trying to corral men into monogamy. So that fear is misplaced and destructive to our own attempts to connect with women.

On top of this, making plans or connecting can feel vulnerable, due to fears of rejection or hard emotions. But expressing interest, while vulnerable, is a thing women appreciate. It will keep them around. Once we learn to trust that women are actually on the same page as us, we can let go of these misplaced defensive maneuvers.

This also applies to lightweight or occasional relationships. A number of women I've dated I've seen only once every month or two. But we would stay solid in our plans and connection practices even with such a small time commitment. I would hold dates months ahead on the calendar. We would go to the same social events and would be friendly there, acknowledging each other as lovers. Staying connected did not require a lot of time or effort. With responsibility and consistency, these connections have often lasted across years.

NEGOTIATING STI CONVERSATIONS

←‑ ‑ ‑ ‑ ‑ ‑ ‑ ‑ ‑ ‑ →

Conversations about sexually transmitted infections (STIs) are one of the major points of pain in nonmonogamy. These conversations are necessary but can be difficult because sex may depend on them. Sometimes being honest about one's STI status or risk factors will lead to no sex or limited sex acts. On top of that, there is a ton of fear and prejudice in the culture around STIs. The stigma is so deep that a person can feel ashamed to even get tested or have STI conversations. Disclosing an actual STI, or risk factors for having one, is much worse. This is a subject where I see lots of men having trouble being authentic, though truly STIs are hard for everyone—most people have had integrity failures around STI discussions at one time or another.

HAVING THE CONVERSATIONS

Good conversations about STIs are necessary for good nonmonogamy—they are how we manage risk and prevent transmission. People want to make well-informed choices where they balance their STI risk against the reward of sexual connection. Doing so requires talking about STI status and risk in an up-front and relaxed manner. As it turns out, the nonmonogamous dating market abundance makes it pretty easy to find interested people with compatible risk-management strategies no matter your current STI situation or risk.

In the nonmonogamy community, speaking easily and frankly about your STI situation leads to more action rather than less! You are demonstrating trustworthiness, which helps put people at ease around *their* STI concerns. Put aside shame and fear and talk matter-of-factly. Practice having these conversations.

In my scene, a standard pre-sex STI conversation includes both or all people describing:

→ Any STIs they might have, including "minor" STIs like HSV-1, HPV, molluscum, or scabies.

→ When they were last tested and what for, and what the results were.

→ What boundaries they want to hold, or physical barriers they want to use, in play situations.

These conversations are expected by all new lovers. I have gotten good at having this conversation quickly, because it often happens at sex parties between the flirting and the having-sex portions of the evening. These conversations may seem unsexy at first, but you should learn the skill of speaking directly about STIs. If you avoid the conversation, or act embarrassed or defensive about having it, you will drive away potential lovers.

In preparation for such conversations, you should read up on STIs, their effects, and their transmission vectors. This is so you can set your boundaries correctly for your level of risk acceptance, and adjust them appropriately if someone else has a particular STI (which will happen occasionally as you date) or if you carry one yourself. People's boundaries can range from no sex at all to no limits at all but usually end up in the middle, with certain sex acts available, with barriers. It is certainly fine to take your time making decisions about having sex with someone who has an STI, but it is really good to decide in advance what your response would be. Things can get kind of hot and confused in the moment, and I've often seen people take risks they would not if they had decided beforehand. Also, if you are getting into situations where you could quickly move from flirting to sex (say, at sex parties), it is considered good form to have your decisions premade, so you can deliver a relaxed yes, no, or yes-with-limits in the moment.

Along with STIs, you should think about and talk about pregnancy. I often see men assume that women will handle any pregnancy concerns, to the point of having unprotected intercourse with women they barely know. This is very foolish and can lead to unplanned pregnancies and possibly children. Take responsibility for pregnancy prevention by always using condoms correctly, considering male birth control as it becomes available, and perhaps limiting your sex acts. Ask your sexual partners about any birth control they are using and what their plan is if birth control fails as part of your standard STI conversations.

GROUP CONVERSATIONS ABOUT STIs

Some of the hardest STI conversations are the ones that involve more than two people. Often this is a couple making decisions about their limits with each other and outside connections, but such conversations happen in most non-monogamous arrangements. Remember that STIs do not care who is primary, and that they can be transmitted in any sexual direction. So everyone should know what's going on, and have a voice. Consult with all others who will be affected by your decisions. When I change my own STI practices I currently check in with a number of other people. The decision is my own, but they all have input.

Group conversations about setting STI limits are often difficult. For example, a lot of couples see intercourse without a condom as special to them, yet they want to require *other* people they have sex with to use condoms with anyone else they have sex with. Negotiations over who gets to have sex without a condom can be fraught, and people tend to turn to hierarchy or power games to get their way, which damages relationships. It is important to step away from hierarchy and give everyone involved a say in what they desire sexually and what their risk management practices will be. Look for creative solutions, like rotating who gets to have sex without a condom while minimizing risk through continued testing and discussion. Strive for consensus, but in the end, give people the agency to make their own risk decisions.

One good tactic is helping people understand how the risks flow through the network of lovers. For example, telling a partner, "If you do contract this STI from this person who has it, I will likely want to stop doing this particular sex act with you to avoid getting infected myself." This approach of having everyone set their personal boundaries around hypothetical events lets people make their own risk decisions while still respecting the risk calculations of their partners.

CONDOMS AND OTHER BARRIERS

Major alert for nonmonogàmous people with a penis: *you have to use condoms* if you want intercourse, whether it's vaginal or anal. It is the standard in nonmonogamous communities. Everyone expects them for intercourse and expects you to be fine with wearing them. Never pressure women to have sex without a condom. It is coercive, word will get around, and you will become a pariah.

Some men have trouble with sensitivity and erections using condoms, or got conditioned to sex without condoms during their monogamous years. It turns out that condoms are a skill like any other aspect of sex and relationships. If you like intercourse, do what it takes to get used to them. That might mean spending time masturbating with condoms or seeing a sex therapist. It may mean getting good with cock rings, playing with your sensitivity levels, taking erection drugs, or whatever it takes. There are a lot of avenues to make condoms work. Also, learn to value non-intercourse sex (oral, manual, kink, etc.). Broadening your focus to non-intercourse sex is a good idea in general. Your partners will appreciate it.

Similarly, accept whatever limits your partners want to set or barriers they want to use. Your goal is to work with their desires and your own, to come up with acts that both you and they are enthusiastic about. Enthusiastic sex is the best sex! Failing to do so gets coercive, which is immoral and harmful. Some women will want you to wear condoms for blow jobs—do so, or skip blow jobs. Some women will want gloves. Other women will want to restrict sex acts to particular acts. Do these things. It will make you a better person. Not coincidentally, it will also lead you to have more and better sex.

LETTING GO OF SEXUAL ENTITLEMENT

There are various ways that sexism gets into how we think about and do sex, and these can be amplified by nonmonogamy. Working past them is the right thing to do. As mentioned, nonmonogamous women are less likely to put up with an unequal or unsatisfying sex life. Unequal or harmful sex practices survive due to women's culturally prescribed ignorance about pleasurable sex, and in nonmonogamous circles that ignorance tends to disappear. So let's talk about how to negotiate, balance, and expand our sexual practices.

Western culture hands men a lot of privileges regarding sex with women. Porn and sexual advertising have historically been aimed at a male audience and men acquire bad misconceptions from them. The sex acts that are considered normal and proper are the sex acts that are most pleasurable for men. Women's desires have tended to be ignored or devalued. This leads to a lot of non-pleasurable, painful, or even violating sex for women, poisoning the experience for everyone.

ESTABLISHING SEXUAL BALANCE

You should balance your sexual practices by making sure they are mutual. The women you are with should enjoy them as much as you. You will both become better lovers and help make the world a better place. Mostly this means listening to the women in your life and trying what they say they like. But I want to call out some particular sexual entitlement difficulties.

First, if there is a sex act you like but you would not want to reverse, that is a red flag you should look at. It's pretty easy to find men who expect blow jobs but refuse to go down on women—these men are bad lovers. If you watch straight porn you might get the idea that most women like receptive anal sex but men never take it in the ass, which is simply not true. If you want to play with women's asses, a great starting point is playing with your own anus or having partners do so. Experiencing anal play helps you understand what feels good or not.

Establishing sexual balance also requires looking at the context around sex. I know a lot of men who are very interested in having threesomes with two women, but do not want threesomes with a woman and another man. This is a hypocrisy to get over. You will find that women are much more open to threesomes with other women if they have been able to enjoy the attention of two men and can expect to do so in the future. Similarly, while kinky people are often solid in their top or bottom roles, experiencing the other side will go a long way towards making you a better kinky lover.

DIVERSIFYING SEX ACTS

One strong piece of male entitlement is the continual elevation of penis-in-vagina (PIV) intercourse as the most important sexual act. Most men greatly enjoy PIV sex (though some do not), but many women do not get much pleasure from it, and some experience PIV sex as painful. Many women do not orgasm from PIV sex by itself. When PIV sex is thought of as the only real sex, it is at the expense of women's pleasure.

Sex toys work well for some women, including vibrators and dildos. Lots of women only orgasm (or orgasm strongly) with vibrators. A lot of men are intimidated by vibrators and dildos, presumably because these tools do things they cannot. Get past this. As with any tools, you learn to use them as an extension of your own body. A guy who can skillfully wield a dildo and vibrator in the bedroom is a guy that many women will want to be in bed with. Also, learning to enjoy women using toys on themselves is just part of being a good lover.

Enjoying non-PIV sex and using sex toys are part of an important dynamic: taking turns. Part of the mythology of heterosexual sex is that it needs to be mutual and all at once—dominant ideology considers simultaneous orgasm to be the holy grail. But learning to take turns opens us up to a more flexible range of pleasures. I think that men (or more generally, people with flesh penises) often have trouble taking turns because erections can be difficult to maintain across an on-again-off-again sexual session. But get away from the need to maintain an erection at all times. Maybe you have an erection and an orgasm at the beginning, and then you have a good long session working with your partner on her pleasure. Perhaps you leave your erection until later. Or maybe it comes and goes, which is also fine.

EXAMINING OUR SEXUALITY

If all of this sounds a bit queer, that's because it is. Mainstream heterosexual sex is a narrow set of acts, and anything outside of these acts has been designated as deviant. Queer people have had a lot more space for experimentation, egalitarian sexual dynamics, and overall a more playful and adaptable sexuality. Queer culture is a source of practical advice that straight people can learn from. It is no accident that many famous sex advice columnists are queer. Often, internalized homophobia keeps men from expanding their sexuality with women. If you feel that having your butt touched makes you gay, or you have absorbed other such myths, work your way past them. They are only limiting you. And homophobia of any sort is very unattractive to most nonmonogamous people.

Overall, straight men tend to avoid examining their own sexuality and sexual urges. Whenever someone brings up a political aspect of sexuality (say, that men receive more pleasure), I see a lot of men try to shut down or avoid the conversation. I think they fear that they will look at the sex they are having and discover that they are being unfair and need to change. But the path of change is something to embrace rather than fear. An examined and adaptable sexuality will lead to more pleasure for you and will make you a better lover and a better person.

ENTHUSIASTIC SEXUAL CONSENT

Good relationships and sexual connections are built on a solid foundation of consent. Consent seems simple on the face of it—only engage in acts that other people have agreed to. But things become intricate as we move past the basic "giving permission" consent model and enter an enthusiastic-consent model. Thinking of consent in terms of enthusiasm is important because the best (most moral and most fulfilling) sex happens when everyone is doing what they enthusiastically want to do. In our culture women are taught to say yes to whatever men want sexually; it can be very hard for women to speak up for their own urges or set boundaries. So it is easy to end up coercing a woman into a sexual act and not even know this is happening. This is harmful to the woman, and she will be much less interested in seeing you in the future. Negotiating enthusiastic consent is crucial to healthy sex.

NEGOTIATING SEXUAL DESIRES

When you are headed towards first-time sex with a woman, ask her open-ended questions, in order to give her space to tell you about her desires: "How do you get turned on (or off)?" "How do you like to be touched?" "What do you prefer to do in bed?" "How do you like to have orgasms, if you want to have orgasms?" This is a great start, though understand that you probably will not hear the entire story in the first conversation. If someone has desires that are unconventional or stigmatized, you may have to build up trust before they tell you. In early sexual encounters, some women prefer things that are more external and feel less vulnerable—perhaps hand sex, oral sex, or nonsexual kink ahead of vaginal or anal intercourse. Beyond sexual acts, it is good to talk about dynamics: rough versus gentle, fast versus slow, sensual versus carnal, and so on. Giving a woman the space to speak first about her desires helps her share them.

After you have heard from her, introduce your own desires that match. Do not press for acts outside her preferences, or acts that might be challenging on a first encounter. You may get there eventually (or not), but the first round is usually a time to connect rather than explore. Aiming for challenging sexual adventures right away can easily fall over into nonconsensual sex. Being the best lover you can be means finding exciting options within the set of your partner's preferences.

The ideal sexual negotiation is one where both (or all) involved bring their own interests to the table, and what actually happens is in the overlapping interests. For example, maybe you have one person who likes to do A and B, really prefers C, is down to do D on occasion to please a partner, and is a solid no to E and F. Maybe another person likes C and D, really likes B and E, and is not down for A or F. If these two people get together a number of times, we hope that they end up doing a lot of B and C with occasional forays into D. This probably sounds like a complex matching problem. That's because it is! But getting used to these conversations makes them really easy and quick, even in chaotic venues like sex parties. Our culture tells us to be silent or ashamed around our sexual interests but a healthy sex life requires breaking past those barriers and negotiating sexual and sensual connections within everyone's desires.

All of the above also extends to long-term connections. Even when two or more people have a well-established sexual history, it is important to check in frequently with a question such as "What are you feeling into?" Sometimes people are feeling a certain way on a certain day. Also, desires and sensual dynamics between people change over time, and it is too easy to stay in an established pattern even as the sensual acts become boring, uncomfortable, or even violating. Regular check-ins will help you adapt to any changes and explore new desires.

AVOIDING DISAPPOINTMENT

Good consent requires putting aside disappointment when a particular sexual act is not available or a particular connection does not work out. Reality often falls short of our fantasies. That's not a problem. I think the feeling that it is a disaster comes from our monogamous cultural training, where either you convince your one partner into a sex act, or it does not happen. Such convincing can easily become coercive, which is to say nonconsensual and harmful. But if we are nonmonogamous, we have less cause for resentment; there can be others who want a particular thing we want. Part of this practice is approaching each connection without high expectations or fantasies, and taking it for what it is rather than what you wish it was. Real magic happens *within* the space of our boundaries.

Sometimes two people are just not erotically compatible. That is okay. Nonmonogamy opens up space for all sorts of valuable non-mainstream relationships, including deep platonic connections. People in long-term relationships may find themselves having no sex, sporadic sex, or sex limited to certain acts. That's fine too. Companionship and friendship are also important in relationships, and we do not value them as much as we should.

WHEN CONSENT IS BROKEN

Sometimes we screw up and violate someone's boundaries. This can happen by mistake, because we acted maliciously, or because we care more about our own pleasure than about not harming another. If you have violated others' boundaries because you want to do harm or do not care, you should immediately stop doing harm and get help. You have bigger problems than I can address here.

If you violate someone's consent by mistake or thoughtlessness, there are things you can and should do, which we will talk about in a moment. Consent is a complex thing, and from time to time most good people accidentally screw it up in minor ways, sometimes major ways. You will likely face situations where you find out (usually afterward) that you crossed a boundary and may have harmed someone. This can happen because someone failed to speak up, or someone misunderstood something, or because one or both of you were tired or intoxicated.

I see men who have broken someone's boundaries often get defensive and fall back on their own recollection of the situation. Worse, men will often deny the accusation and try to convince the woman she's wrong. But remember that your experiences and memories are subjective. It is important to step back from any defensiveness you may feel and move into a space of taking responsibility and being caring. The most important thing is that a person has been hurt. Even an accidental violation can cause significant emotional distress and residual trauma. Being compassionate means taking care of the person and addressing the harm as best you can. This is no different from any other mistake—if you screw up and hurt people or create a bad situation, defensiveness only makes things worse. The initial violation may have been accidental harm but following that violation with defensiveness can re-traumatize the hurt person, which is then purposeful harm.

Unfortunately, mainstream culture promotes defensiveness rather than apology or reconciliation when it comes to consent issues. Our culture tends to dismiss the woman as crazy or making things up, which makes it easy for *you* to dismiss women who say you have harmed them. The epidemic of rape has raised the moral stakes for any consent violation, and possibly the legal stakes too, though actual convictions are rare. Still, defensiveness will only make things worse. Taking responsibility and collaborating about making amends will improve the situation for everyone, yourself included.

You can accept someone else's experience while still holding your own experience. Do not confess to things that do not match your own experience of memory but accept that whatever exactly happened, you have indeed caused a person harm, so act from a place of compassion, and try to make amends.

If someone tells you that you have broken their consent, believe them. They are the arbiters of what *their* consent means. It was probably pretty bad for them if they are even willing to bring it up. Try to approach the situation from a place of curiosity. Listen to them about their experience and try to figure out what went wrong. This information is a gift that will help you empathize and avoid a repeat experience.

You may hear about the boundary violation through a third party, and you should be comfortable with working through a mediator. Often people are (quite reasonably!) unwilling to talk directly to someone who has crossed their boundaries.

Apologizing and asking if there are amends you can make can be scary because you are giving someone else leverage over you. But people tend to be very reasonable around asking for amends. You should agree to them, including requests that are difficult for you. Someone may ask you to leave a particular social scene for a long period of time. The compassionate thing is to grant that request. Acting compassionately will serve you much better in the long term than selfishness in the short term.

Nonmonogamous men are often worried about what a consent accusation will do to their reputation and position in their communities. Reputation in small communities is very important. However, this is not your first concern, right? Any harm to community standing does not compare to the harm directly caused by consent violations, which really mess people up. If you miss a couple parties or whatever, it is no big deal compared to someone else's months of nightmares, difficulty being sexual or touching others, difficulty trusting partners, and so on.

If you admit to an accidental consent violation and work to make amends, there will probably be no ill effects to your standing. I have found that people are extremely forgiving and understanding if you deal with the situation with a good heart. Acting compassionately and taking responsibility makes you a better person and people will respond accordingly.

Consent violations happen in all directions and with any gender. While men face boundary violations less often, your own consent may be broken at some point, and that may be traumatizing for you. It is always hard to speak up when boundaries have been crossed. The most important thing is to take care of yourself, find ways to be validated, and work on healing in whatever way works. Try to find and speak to people who will believe your experience. It is very easy to drop down into a spiral of shame and self-doubt when one's boundaries are crossed. If it feels good to bring it up directly with the person who broke your consent, then do that. If it feels good to have someone else work on communicating what happened, then do that. If you want to just talk to friends about it, do that. If you want to let it lie, then do that, though be aware that suppressed trauma often comes out in subtle and difficult ways later. Take care of yourself and believe in your own feelings.

SUPPORTING WOMEN AROUND ABUSE AND SEXUAL ASSAULT

In order to connect deeply with women, we need to connect with the reality that women are disproportionately at risk of rape, sexual harassment, and relationship abuse, and they know it.

The harms of rape-supportive culture come in many forms, from the horrific to the seemingly-minor-but-still-bad. Nonconsensual touching, groping, and grabbing happen both out in the world and inside supposedly safe communities. Rape is sometimes by strangers but more often by someone a woman knows. Sexual assault often arises from an escalation of agreed-upon activities. Western culture has a thousand ways to undermine the consent, emotional boundaries, and physical boundaries of women. Among them are the myths that women have worth only for sex, dating, or marriage, that women will be available to men who pressure them enough, that women have few sexual desires of their own, that women act as gatekeepers for men's sexual desires, that women will be highly compliant once in a relationship, that women enjoy performing emotional labor, and that women are sexual followers instead of leaders, among others. These ideas circulate constantly in the culture and in media narratives, creating real danger for women, who are reasonably fearful as a result.

The ever-present possibility of harm subtly poisons relationships between men and women. Mixed-gender nonmonogamy is less popular than between gay men, for instance, because sexual freedom is associated with harm to women. This association pushes women away from nonmonogamy, especially when nonmonogamous communities are not strongly, visibly anti-rape and anti-abuse. Women who feel like they have to constantly police their physical boundaries will often have trouble opening up to other people. Women who feel (correctly) that nonmonogamy might mark them as available for harassment or rape may avoid it for that reason. If you are ever frustrated at how difficult it can be to connect with defensive women, do not blame women. The true target of your frustration is *rape culture*.

To successfully support women around issues of abuse and sexual assault, we need to learn certain skills. Our culture does not teach these skills, and in fact teaches us to dismiss women or support abuse. So our instincts are often bad even when we want to be supportive. To move towards fixing this, I encourage you to do your research. Find feminist and anti-rape resources and read them. Read essays about consent, abuse, and sexual assault. Once you have a handle on the depths, move towards an anti-abuse stance in your personal and public life. If you were making rape jokes or otherwise making light of abuse, stop. Instead, speak out about how abuse and rape are serious issues in your social circles and in public. As much as possible, transmit and amplify things that women (particularly survivors) have to say on these topics.

LISTENING TO WOMEN IN OUR LIVES

One way we can be immediately effective in battling rape culture is by supporting the women around us. Every woman has faced some level of sexual harassment or coercion in her life. Rape is frequent enough that around one in six women in your social world have been sexually assaulted. If you have dated more than a handful of women, you have probably dated one or more survivors, who probably did not tell you about their history.

Sooner or later someone in your life will tell you about a sexual assault or abusive relationship they have been through. If you start speaking out against abuse in your social circles, you are much more likely to hear about such problems. When you indicate a good understanding, people who have kept quiet start opening up.

Listen and believe them. I have heard numerous reports and have yet to have someone lie to me. It is well-known that false rape reports are incredibly rare. And yet we often hesitate to believe that someone (often whom we know and like) could do what we are hearing. People are often not as noble as we would like, and some do really harmful things. Put aside your need to think well of people and listen to what you are hearing. Engage your curiosity and active-listening skills, and avoid leaping to conclusions or naming things for the speaker. Your goal here is to understand and validate the experience this person went through. Curiosity and receptivity is how to get there.

Emotional abuse is a trickier violation to define than physical abuse. Emotional abuse is controlling behavior, manipulation, or other tactics to coerce or gain control over another. Many of these tactics undermine the self-esteem and agency of the abused person: isolation, denigration, intimidation, emotional blackmail, and so on. One tactic of emotional abuse is *gaslighting*: trying to convince someone that they are crazy or otherwise should not trust their own perceptions and memories, and should trust you instead. It can be very hard to see emotional abuse happening. Unlike consent violations or domestic violence, often there is no particular act that obviously crosses a boundary. Someone may not realize they are being emotionally abused until it has been going on for a long time or until after a relationship has ended.

However, emotional abuse is usually very damaging and creates trauma similar to physical violations. Emotional abuse seems to be the more common form in nonmonogamous communities because it is easier to hide than physical abuse. If you are hearing about emotional abuse, believe that it is happening. If *you* are being emotionally abused, trust your instincts around what feels harmful to you. Never dismiss an instance of emotional abuse as not real—doing so replicates the tactics of that abuse and re-traumatizes people. Instead, understand that emotional abuse is a complex and subtle thing.

A goal of these conversations is validation. If what you are hearing sounds terrible, express sympathy and acknowledge that it sounds terrible. By the time such things rise to the level of actual conversations, significant harm has usually already happened. Holding empathy for that harm is one of the most supportive things you can do. Whether or not you personally agree with what a person is saying, their *experience* is their own, and validating it is the most caring path you can take. It is not your job to adjudicate fault or discern the real truth of what has happened. Your job is to be as caring and sympathetic as possible to someone who is feeling wounded.

Beyond conversation, you should offer whatever support you can to survivors. Sometimes they may want you to mediate. Sometimes they want to warn other vulnerable members of a social circle. They may want to exclude the person who has hurt them from events, or otherwise set up safety for themselves. Try to aid them as you can, while still taking care of yourself.

BUILDING ANTI-ABUSE COMMUNITY

Often a sexual assault, consent violation, or abusive relationship will divide a community as details come out. The accused person may mobilize all their social resources to silence or discredit their accuser. When someone engages in social manipulation or harassment to defend themselves against an accusation, this is a sign that they are malicious—possibly malicious enough to have committed the thing they are accused of. There is often lying or counter-accusations involved. Support the original accuser (who is usually the person with less power), even if this comes at personal cost to you. I think people often have the urge to "avoid drama," "stay neutral," or "be fair," to the detriment of supporting the survivor. There is no neutral stance here, because the supposedly neutral stance actually defaults to tolerating rape and abuse. If you want to reduce harm, you must take a consistent and proactive stand for the survivor to be heard.

Sometimes these fights escalate to a point where they split or destroy entire communities. This often happens when the accused person is charismatic, well-liked, or a community leader. People with a lot of social capital will often maliciously mobilize it against an accuser. If the person being called out is a charismatic leader in a community, you should suspect them *more* rather than less. While most leaders are totally fine, people who seek to abuse, control, or rape others tend to purposefully seek positions of power. Such a person can easily poison or destroy entire communities.

Leaders should be held to a high standard around how they treat people in their personal life. You should expect any community leader, organizer, or educator to take a strong anti-abuse stance, including taking action when issues come up. If they do not, it means they are creating and running an unsafe community. Such leaders should not be leading, and you should try to remove them from power.

Within nonmonogamous communities, the gossip network (or "information-sharing network") is a crucial part of how women protect themselves. After all, the police and legal system are often useless or actually dangerous to members of minority communities. So sharing information is the main way that women figure out whom to trust and whom to fear. Don't put down women's information sharing as harmful gossip or dismiss it as causing drama. Do not be shy about sharing information, naming names, or making public statements about particular people who have caused harm. Holding a nonmonogamous person truly accountable for harmful actions often means having their entire community hold them accountable. Having word get around can halt a person from causing further harm, even if they are in a leadership position. Being open and transparent can bring more cases out of the woodwork, clarifying the problem. Abuse and consent violations thrive in an atmosphere of silence and misinformation, but they are stopped by acknowledgment and exposure.

Learning to engage with these issues will help you make the world a better place, and will bring you closer to the women around you. When a number of people visibly take an anti-abuse and pro-consent stance in a community, the whole community can become much safer and more trusting.

CONCLUSION: SEEKING PARADISE

For many of us, the journey into nonmonogamy is a quest to reach a better place. A place where we are free to express ourselves with others who appreciate us. A place where we are not isolated, but form an abundance of connections. A place where we are actually satisfied with the connections in our lives.

I see many nonmonogamous men searching. Perhaps it's because we externalize the journey into nonmonogamy into a quest for a magical life or magical people. But we can only get so much from outside ourselves. So we end up searching, searching, searching, and never quite finding.

All the time I see men looking, but they are somehow not searching in the right way, and doors stay closed to them. I have probably done more of this fruitless searching than you ever will. At least, I hope so. Men ask me where the really good parties are, but the party is good if you make it good, and it is bad if you make it bad. I see guys who are disrespectful towards women, and then wonder why women don't stay around. I see men who act selfish or self-centered and then wonder why no one is generous towards them. I see guys who do not seek to understand the women around them, and then wonder why no one seems to understand them. I see men who do not make the effort to stay connected, and then wonder why their connections fall apart. I see guys looking here, there, and everywhere for magic to happen, not realizing that magic is not something you find, it's something you create.

We men have been fed a pile of lies that make it hard to have good relationships, and harder to have successful nonmonogamous relationships. The dominant culture is at fault for convincing us that the solutions we seek are outside ourselves. In the movies, real men solve their relationship problems by going out and saving the day, rather than by having hard conversations. Men in the movies get women by stubbornly pursuing them, rather than by thinking about what they want and what women want. We are bombarded with a masculinity that is withdrawn, isolated, impenetrable, neglectful, uncompromising, and competitive. This is terrible for forming personal connections. Most of us have already expanded beyond such culture-approved masculinity, but if we want to be successful in nonmonogamy, we need to go farther. We need to be outgoing, connected, vulnerable, nurturing, compromising, and collaborative.

We feel like the answers are tantalizingly close, yet we search outside ourselves. The answer is not in finding the right community, meeting the right woman, saying the right thing, or putting on the right image. These things help, but the important answers and obstacles turn out to be mostly inside ourselves. This is why they always feel so close.

Self-change is the answer. Then all the other dominoes will fall: we will say the right things and make the right connections and find the best communities. Paradise is not out there somewhere—paradise is here inside us, waiting.

With this book, I am trying to send you postcards from paradise. While I still certainly have hard times, and will always have more self-work to do, I am living in my own nonmonogamous utopia. I have trust that I can have all the things I want in my dating life, and that my path is solid. After so much failure, it took me a decade of success before I really started believing in it. I am surrounded by other men who are making nonmonogamy work for them in spectacular ways.

I want to tell you that you can find your way to non-monogamous paradise. The path is convoluted and often difficult, and the paradise you arrive in will probably not look like the one you set out to find. But nonmonogamous success is very real, and you have everything you need to achieve it—you just have to do the work to make it happen. I hope you find your nonmonogamous dream, perhaps someday soon.

ACKNOWLEDGMENTS

This book would not have been possible without the review and editing work, emotional labor, and patience of the people around me. I would like to thank the people close to me who read drafts and provided edits: Ariana Waynes, Jade, Jennifer Arter, Jon Spinner, and Laura Thomas. I am so appreciative of my partners who were incredibly patient and forgiving with me during a difficult writing process, and who did not break up with me: Ariana Waynes, Jade, Jen Day, Laura Thomas, and Sarah Crane Newman. I have a big thank you for my two editors, Alan MacRobert and Hazel Boydell, who put in a ton of work fixing my unnatural prose. I want to thank Kevin Patterson for writing the foreword, and Jetta Rae for consulting on the title and cover copy. And I have the biggest appreciation of all for Eve Rickert, who brought me the idea, was very patient with me through a complex and difficult process, and actually managed to publish this book—thank you so much.

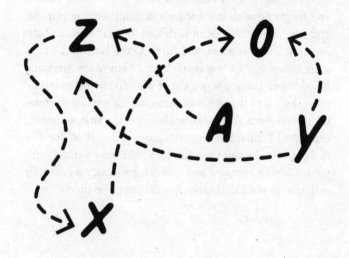

The Pegging Book:
A Complete Guide to Anal Sex with a Strap-On Dildo

Cooper S. Beckett and Lyndzi Miller

"*The Pegging Book* is a wonderful addition to sex ed literature! As an act, pegging has gained popularity among people of all genders, sexual orientations, and ages. It is great to finally have a single resource which teaches how to peg as well as gives it cultural context and history. Beckett and Miller have done justice to a topic which goes so much deeper than a titillating headline! In addition to great content, the book is beautifully illustrated and provides readers with a solid understanding of anatomy and pleasure centers. This is a must-buy for any person looking to understand how to peg or the act's cultural significance."

— Rebecca E. Blanton, writer,
podcaster, and kink educator

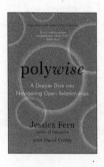

Polywise:
A Deeper Dive into Navigating Open Relationships

Jessica Fern, with David Cooley

"In *Polywise*'s expansive and eye-opening exploration of the possibilities of nonmonogamous life, Jessica Fern invites us to examine our individual and societal beliefs about love and offers an indispensable guide for newly opened couples' transitions to their next chapter. If you are ready to think more deeply about communication, codependency, conflict, and repair in your most important relationships, *Polywise* is required reading. I am looking forward to recommending this guide to clients and students."

— Alexandra H. Solomon, PhD, author of
Love Every Day and host of *Reimagining Love*

Pepper Mint is an activist, educator, and community organizer in the polyamory and BDSM communities in San Francisco.